The Pathless Path

The Pathless Path

God, Grace, Guru

Charles B. Crenshaw, Jr.

Ahymsa Publishing

ISBN 978-1-940629-01-8

Ahymsa Publishers
631 University Ave. N.E.
Minneapolis MN 55413
info@ahymsapublishers.com

Distributed by Lotus Press,
PO Box 325, Twin Lakes, Wisconsin 53181 USA
www.lotuspress.com, 1- 800-824-6396, lotuspress@lotuspress.com

Printed in the USA

Cover and book design: David Spohn (QuarryRoadPress.com)

Table of Contents

Biography

Charles B Crenshaw, Jr. is a yogi, a meditation teacher, an interfaith minister and co-founder of the Inner Peace Yoga Center in Indianapolis, a non-profit educational organization dedicated to teaching yoga science. He has been teaching the science of yoga world-wide since 1985 and continues to train teachers in the ways of the tradition as he was taught by Sri Swami Rama and his leading adherents. He also teaches Eastern religions and critical thinking courses in the College of Humanities and Science at the University of Phoenix. He lives in Indianapolis with his wife Carol.

Acknowledgments

Someone once asked me who my heroes were, so I would like to acknowledge these people first—my mother and father, Dr. Martin Luther King, Jr. and Mahatma Gandhi.

On the more pragmatic side, I would like to thank Swami Veda Bharati and Ahymsa Publishers for publishing the book. Without the publisher's kindness, the book might not have seen the light of day. I would like to thank David Spohn for his cover design and typesetting work, Carolyn Kott Washburne for her proofreading and for the not-so-silent voice of Wesley Van Linda who, believing in the book's significance, helped me to tell the story by managing its publishing. There are not enough thanks for his kindness.

I would like to thank the students at Inner Peace Yoga Center who heard me whisper about this book and took the time to critically read my drafts before publication; none of them is more important to acknowledge than my friend Bonnie Hand. I cannot fail to mention my writers group with their good and often painful feedback on my work. Bethany, Maurice, and Lou, I thank you for your encouragement.

Introduction

Every seeker of truth will arrive at his truth by a path completely original to him/her. These paths traverse the fascinating internal landscapes of our personalities. All that happens in our physical life and in the episodes thereof are reflections and projections of what transpires in the subtle inner world of our mental personalities.

Few are fortunate to be endowed with clarity to perceive the connections between the inner world and the ever-changing outer circumstances. These fortunate ones then can chart their paths, or rather, the paths get charted for them, as an act of grace from forces invisible; some misname these events 'coincidences'.

Charles Crenshaw's story of his 'seeking and finding' is an example of this truth. He has managed to synchronize his inner and outer world by the grace of the forces that have played a subtly dominant role in driving his life's chariot around all the curves of life's mysteries.

Those who read this work will learn how one may also chart one's path, to respond to the inner messengers about paths to be taken in the outer world.

One is born with all one's answers already written in his/her soul. The question of questions is how to read those answers. Charles Crenshaw has been taught the art of reading those answers, some of which he presents in this immensely readable work.

Even though I have known Charles Crenshaw for well over twenty years, his book reveals his deep spiritual discoveries, and even more so, his discoveries about the unique spiritual master whom we share.

Following Charles' example, may readers follow their own gently curving paths around mountains of questions until eventually, beautiful vistas of answers are revealed. Readers' individual journeys of 'seeking and finding' will resonate as they turn the pages of this magnetic book.

Swami Veda Bharati,
Disciple of Swami Rama of the Himalayas.
Rishikesh, India

I pay homage to those who have been most graciously set before us to point the way to the light: Christ, the Buddha, Krishna, the Prophet, my Gurudev, the lineage of gurus that produced him, and all the saints and sages, male and female, past and present, theistic in their orientation or not. May any positive benefit created by this effort be reserved for all sentient beings in each of the ten cardinal directions.

CHAPTER ONE

Entering the Light of Wisdom

*It's 1978—these people are leftovers from the sixties, hippies—*this was my impression of the two people who ran the vegetarian cafe. They were as odd to me as I was to them, hardly two years from active duty in the Navy, sitting, eating a veggie burger at their café. The lunch hours I spent hanging around this little café, so small it hardly had a name, were always interesting. Located in the newly renovated City Market, this café without walls was just across the street from where I worked.

A year since I began transitioning to a vegetarian diet, this little café had popped up just in time. It was a gem in Indianapolis for would-be vegetarians. The U.S., not being a Mecca for vegetarians at the time, didn't have very many cafés like this anywhere. My dietary experiments, eating all raw food for months on end, fasting for days on juices, or without taking anything at all, were all for the sake of some unknown quest, and this little café brought some much-needed sanity to my bizarre food regimen.

The café, bordered on three sides by a counter, had as its back wall a railing that protected it from falling down onto the main floor of the Market. Customers of the market would stand, as I would sit on my stool while at the café, and look out over the bustling main floor of the market. You found some of everything at the market, from a health food store to lunchtime jazz on Fridays. The market's smells reminded me of excursions I'd made with my dad in my youth. The order of the day then was a big beef hot dog with all the trimmings from one of the regular vendors. The veggie burgers, patted together right before my eyes, were part of my effort at eating healthy and being kind to the planet.

The café and the people who operated it now seem like dream characters, all too quirky to have really existed. The lithesome blonde co-owner, Mary Beth, was pleasant, but there was something different about her that I couldn't put my finger on. I noticed it as she patted the ingredients into the veggie burgers, and moved about the café's small square footage. I wasn't sure if this had to do with the hippie side of her personality or this thing she was always mentioning—hatha yoga. Her husband, Joey, was a thin man who truly looked like a hippie, with his frayed, bell-bottoms and tie-dyed shirt and curly dark hair. When he was there, he always moved about the space frenetically. I could tell, as they'd say in the neighborhood, that this guy was working hard to keep his hustle going. Mary Beth on the other hand appeared calmer. Maybe it was because she was a nursing mother, or because of this thing, hatha yoga.

My conversations with Mary Beth and Joey centered around my interest in meditation. I always found a sympathetic ear with these hippies. *They were hippies; they ought to have known something about this,* I thought to myself. I didn't know why, but they tolerated my musings, and I was thankful. I had been practicing meditation for six years, self-taught from a little book I treasured. One afternoon Mary Beth looked at me as she played with her cherub-faced baby, who was sitting in a carrier on the table behind the counter.

She asked me, "Charles? Do you know much about yoga?"

"Yeah, I know about it. It's something that women do for exercise in this country. I'm more familiar with karate and Tai Chi. I started studying karate in the service, but I gravitated to Tai Chi. This is the stuff that men do for exercise related to yoga."

"That's what you think yoga is?"

"Well, yeah. I've run across the word yoga in my little book, but it's got nothing to do with this thing you do." I knew by now that Mary Beth was a hatha yoga teacher. "Yoga related to meditation has something to do with joining your mind to the infinite, and not this thing that you do," I said, proud of my proclamation.

Mary Beth just laughed and went about amusing little Chrissie. I would get chuckles or odd looks whenever I talked to people about meditation. People would give me that look that said, "What you need to do is go to church or something." It was for this reason that I kept my thoughts and my comments to myself, but there was something different about Mary Beth's asking and her laugh.

Mary Beth wiped down the counter, removing the crumbs of an earlier customer, wiping her way around the counter and back to me. "You might like to look into this," she said as she handed me a flier from underneath the counter.

It read **Sri Swami Rama of the Himalayas coming to Indianapolis.** The finer print said: Rama was raised in a cave in the Himalayas, and in his youth taught Buddhist scriptures.

Seeing the ad, all I could think of was swamis, Woodstock, people sitting around the floor sucking on a hubbly-bubbly filled with hashish or dropping a hit of acid. I didn't have time for that.

The sixties, just a few years past, had been filled with turmoil. I'd spent four years of my life in the Navy since. There, the old salts sat around debating the benefits of alcohol over marijuana or psychedelics while they consumed fifths of hard liquor, destroying their livers. Neither of the choices for mind-altering substances made any real sense to me anymore.

"No thanks," I said to Mary Beth, handing the flier back to her so she could save it for some other aspiring space cadet.

"Remember now, you told me that you have been practicing meditation."

"Yeah, I've been getting along pretty well on my own for these past few years."

"Have you ever had a teacher?"

I shook my head a bit dejectedly.

"No? Then how do you know you're getting along well?

She had a point. Because I lived alone, no one really knew what I was doing. With my meditation, I always felt like someone lurking in the shadows, practicing some forbidden art. Certainly I could have used some guidance, but it didn't seem like I was going to get anything useful from someone listed on a brochure in this funky little café.

Meditation was a habit I had acquired while away in the service. Going into the service had been the best and the worst thing I ever did. On the down side, after returning home as a veteran, my ways were classified as "crazy." Still, knowing I had much to learn about meditation, I didn't feel there was anyone in Indianapolis, at least no one trustworthy, who knew anything more about meditation than I did.

I went back and forth about going to see the man mentioned on the flier. Every day at lunch it lay there on the counter, but Mary Beth never mentioned it again. Long disillusioned by the religion of my birth, its conditioning still haunted me. My mind ran all the options: *Are you really expecting this swami to provide you any real answers you chump? Shouldn't you be finding some Christian who knows about these things or something? You know you are going to hell for even having this interest, don't you? Ahhh—I don't buy hell anymore anyway!*

I could manufacture arguments like this forever, but here's an opportunity, if this man was authentic, to meet someone who could certainly know something that I had only read about in books.

I hoped. After long and tormenting internal dialogue, over several weeks, I found myself in the basement conference room of a near north side bank sitting in an audience of normal looking people waiting to hear this man, this swami.

The swami, a handsome, tall, brown man, with a very erect posture, looked very chic in his tan Nehru suit. He spoke in a commanding voice.

"The breath is the link between the mind and the body." He broke up his talk with demonstrations using volunteers from the audience. This all seemed so corny. I hadn't attended this event to see this swami do demonstrations, but then I didn't really know why I attended at all. The swami talked a lot about breathing and relaxation, and then the presentation was over.

Is that it? There has to be more to all this than this lightweight little talk.

The swami asked the audience, "Are there any questions?"

I impatiently listened to the questions, hoping that someone would ask my question and I would glean some insight from this mysterious man, but the questions seemed so elementary. I had so many questions, and nobody to ask. For years I had been studying everything I could get my hands on about meditation. If this man was all Mary Beth and Joey said he was, then he should have some answers for me.

When I realized that no one was going to ask my questions, I blurted out, "What is discriminative awareness?"

"Truth," the swami replied to my question instantly, looking around the room for who had posed the question.

"What is enlightenment?"

"Peace and happiness," was his ready response, as he caught sight of me.

Was this swami really someone I could learn something from, but how would that happen? He was only in Indianapolis for one night.

As the presentation neared its end, the swami mentioned that he was sorry but he had something called initiations that were scheduled. I looked around for my pseudo-hippie friends, hoping they might formally introduce me to the swami, but I couldn't locate them.

As people started to leave, I stood there knowing no one in the dispersing crowd. People milled about him asking him questions, and buying his books at the back of the room. One man in particular was standing in front of the swami, holding a Bible, and making his case about something. The Swami acknowledged him, patted him on the shoulder, and then the man walked away. The swami, alone now, turned to check the lectern for his belongings.

Here's my chance. It's just the swami and me. But what am I going to do, walk up to him and just start talking? "Say swami, I wanna rap with you about a few things." No that won't do. How would he know what I was talking about with all this street lingo?

But I had to do or say something quick; he was going to get away. I wended my way through the maze of chairs in front of me, and as I got within arm's reach of the swami, the words to ask him still hadn't come. *So you lived in a cave? Are you a Buddhist?* With him still turned away from me, I put my right hand on his left shoulder. Still not knowing what I was going to say, I kept rehearsing lines in my mind. The swami turned to his left to begin to face me.

As he turned, the words popped into my mind and moved toward my mouth. "You know swami, I been . . . I been thinking about this . . . this wandering mendicant thing . . . " Little did I know that the man whom I had my hand on had actually lived this sort of life. It didn't matter that I'd stumbled over my words trying to speak to him, all the rest that was in my mind to ask the swami did not reach my lips to become audible.

Standing with my hand on his left shoulder, he turned to face me, his face lit with the expectation of interaction— . . . *my mind . . . what . . . is going . . . on?* Wide-eyed, I'd opened the door to an oven set at broil and walked slow motion, full body, into the blast of heat coming from it. Dazzling, blinding white light accompanied the blast of heat. Every hair on my body stood on end, my face ruffled, as if being hammered by incredibly forceful winds, or so it seemed. I stood there, transfixed. I couldn't breathe, I couldn't escape—*Something . . . is . . . . happening . . . . can't . . . see . . . where . . . swami? . . . where . . . the . . . . room . . . ? . . . . no . . . me . . . mind . . . . . .*

Time meant nothing, it didn't exist, the world did not exist. One second, one minute, one lifetime, an eternity! Consummate bliss!

Some sense of self slowly started to return, and as best I could, I thought to turn away before I was further reduced to some Star Trek-ish mass on the floor, waiting for the molecules to be swept up by the janitor. Unable to turn away, I had no clear vision, it was still disconnected from my brain. The heat dissipated sooner than the light.

As my vision returned and I regained by faculties, I could see that I had turned completely away from where the swami was standing, and I was facing the people sitting at the back of the room selling books and answering questions.

Didn't anyone see what just happened? Wasn't the whole room affected by this?

People were going about the room cleaning up after the event. When I recovered enough to continue my obviously unnoticed interaction with the swami, he was gone.

I walked around the room looking for my café friends, and as before, they were nowhere to be found. I made my way to the parking lot, dazed by the events, talking to people who had been at the lecture, asking them if they noticed anything at the end, without giving away what had just transpired between the swami and me.

In later years, I'd ask my guru, "What was that, what did you do that night?" He always managed to skirt answering this question. The events were left as a mystery to unfold in the life of an earnest seeker. A few unfathomable moments in time, and life, as I thought I knew it, was changed forevermore.

CHAPTER TWO

Just West of the Himalayas

I wasn't raised in a Himalayan cave, or brought up in the mystical land of the Dalai Lama. I grew up literally on the other side of the tracks. Entering the neighborhood from the west involved crossing a wide expanse of railroad tracks; there the neighborhood began.

The street you found after crossing those tracks was bordered by liquor stores and a nightclub, in an area colloquially known as The Corner. Moving east, the neighborhood was filled with single- and double-storied public housing units that bordered single-family dwellings, and a large park.

The smaller area that I grew up in, three-quarters of a mile from those tracks, was called Love Town, because almost everyone within a few blocks' radius was related to one another. Within that range, everybody knew who I was. I couldn't go anyplace in Love Town without someone knowing exactly what I was doing. If I pulled some boyish prank, my parents knew about it before I got home. This would often mean a scolding from a neighbor or relative only to be greeted with the same when I got home, with an added swat or two across the rear from momma, or more, depending on the infraction.

A block or so from our little house was the red-tiled church where Momma took my twin sister and me, her two little nappy-headed sweethearts, when we were just three years old, nine years before the birth of our baby sister. Across the street from the church, and across a big, open drainage ditch that also ran in front of our house, was the public park. This smaller part of the overall neighborhood, in my little mind, was heaven on earth.

Back then, it was endless miles across the local park's open, green expanse to the grade school that everyone in the neighborhood attended. In the park, you could find kiddies swinging, basketball, softball, kickball games, and more. You could as easily witness an Easter Egg hunt, usually supervised by my mother, as you could a game of dice. The entire neighborhood had access to the park, and at times, you could find things more unsettling than the police breaking up dice games.

"Where'd ya get the ice cream?" I asked a group of big boys one day when I was seven or eight.

They were at least seventeen or eighteen years old, and they could curse without anyone telling them they couldn't, or at least so I thought. Without hesitation, the ringleader, Stack, a long, lean boy with a fierce expression, spoke up.

"We stole it off the ice cream truck. You can have some if you want."

My parents and church had taught me that stealing was wrong, but I still didn't know enough to avoid these boys, something my dad would teach me later.

I asked him, "How'd you do that?"

Proudly Stack said, "We just had someone beat on his truck real loud. When he got out to see what was goin' on, one of us got into the truck and threw out the container of ice cream."

"Didn't the ice cream man know it was you who took the ice cream?"

"It don't matter, we ain't afraid of the ice cream man."

I knew they weren't afraid of the ice cream man or the police, but I also thought they were dumb.

"So I bet you rob the bus drivers too, don't ya, huh?"

There had been a rash of bus driver robberies, and I figured these boys were responsible.

Stack grabbed me by the shoulders and sneered, "Yeah, so what if we did? If you tell on us, we'll kick your ass."

"No, no I won't tell," I said, thoroughly frightened by his threat.

For a long time, I firmly believed that the bus companies stopped carrying change in those little coin dispensers and went to exact fare because of these boys in public housing, boys who eventually ended up in prison or dead. In the surrounding neighborhood, there were shootings, numbers running, pimps, car-trunk clothiers, and drugs.

On my errands to the local supermarket, walking past the public housing, I'd see the pimps' Cadillacs with their vinyl tops and sun roofs, and I often wondered what their life was all about. One day I finagled my way into a pimp's apartment.

"What are you doin' here, little man?"

He was laying up in the bed with one of his *ho's,* as he called his women employees.

"I . . . I . . . I just wanted to see."

"To see what? You get the hell outta here." This man knew my mother, and knew there would be hell to pay for indoctrinating me into his peculiar ways.

All I knew about pimps was that they had something to do with sex, and sex made everyone crazy. Sex made people feel guilty and then they joined church to be saved—from sex. At least, that is how it appeared to me.

Over the years, I came to understand that my extended neighborhood was on a black list. Taxi cab drivers were told to be wary, and at one point, no taxis would bring their fares across that wide set of tracks into the neighborhood after dark. As harrowing as it was sometimes, I grew to be a young man in that neighborhood, with unseen hands preparing me for what was to unfold, sheltered and protected as much as possible by my family and what I learned in the church.

Home. Ordinary, mysterious, and fascinating, everything happened within the bounds of our little house and within the confines of its small front and back yard. We lived in a double that my nuclear family shared with my grandfather and paternal aunt and her children, my first cousins. On each side of the double there were three rooms with a bathroom on the first floor, and three bedrooms on the second floor arranged in shotgun fashion, one, two, three.

My childhood, fairly common for a boy like me, was a gift in most ways. It was my extraordinary gift, as a male, to have been born at the same time as a woman—my twin, and to have her as my closest friend and ally during my initial years on earth. Growing up with her forced me to come to grips with things that most men never consider in an entire lifetime. I understood early on that she had this extraordinary capacity that I didn't possess. A soul would pass into her body and out again as a child, a curious thought, but true. There was this fascinating sense of sameness, a sense of unity that I first experienced with my closest friend. This sense transcended the boundaries of our family connection. I discovered that expressing being in harmony, in unity with everything and with everyone, was not the norm. Other than my twin sister, I played with my cousins and other neighborhood kids in the backyard.

A red brick walkway split the yard in half, the side my granddad owned and our side. One sunny day in the backyard, I puzzled a playmate of mine. Sitting in child-sized, vinyl-bound, padded rocking chairs, on their way to the junk heap, I mentioned to my playmate, "Did you know that you and I are both the same?"

I didn't know exactly how to explain what I meant, but the feeling, the knowing that this was the truth, that we were all part of some grand whole, was there.

"No, we aren't!"

"Are too!"

"Are not!"

We went back and forth for some time, as kids do.

Why doesn't he understand what I am saying? Is there something wrong with me?

My young mind grappled with something that seemed to have no place for expression, not even the one place where it seemed it would get support—church.

The church reinforced things taught to me at home, such as respect for my elders and the Golden Rule, but it also confused me with its contradictions about women, about my sister.

The pastor said, "Eve tricked Adam."

I listened innocently, "Eve fed Adam the apple that the serpent beguiled her into eating, and it is Eve that is responsible for man's fall."

In my brief life experience, I was the one of the two of us—my sister, the woman child, and I—who was the troublemaker. I was the initiator of most problem behavior. I naively initiated some painful discussions based on what I was being taught.

"Neenee, you were the cause for why Jesus had to die on the cross?"

My sister, her big beautiful eyes widening at what I said to her, didn't respond. I couldn't feel the hurt behind the look in her eyes, but I knew it hurt her. My mind convulsed in conflict that God would claim that my sister was somehow part cause of the entire world's pain, pain and suffering she had no way of knowing existed. Who knew what I was being prepared for with these stark confrontations with my twin soul?

CHAPTER THREE

In All the Wrong Places

We were all in that room that night with different ideas about what we thought would take place. Everything in my life now hinged on that one fateful meeting. I tried in vain to integrate the experience I had had in that bank basement, but only one bit of information made sense, the piece about physical exercise, something I thought I thoroughly understood after my time in service.

"Can I get a volunteer from the audience?" asked the swami.

An older gentleman moved to the front of the room, and the swami had him lie prostrate on the eight-foot folding table that was situated there.

"Separate your feet, and lower your shoulders down away from your ears."

The wide-eyed elderly man adjusted his suit coat, which he had neglected to remove, and situated his hips so he could conform to the swami's request.

"Now let me have your arm," the swami said, "Just relax."

The swami then attempted several times to just let the man's arm drop on the table alongside where his body lay, but there was always some hesitation.

The swami shook the man's arm and said, "Just relax, let me have your arm. You want to be aware of letting go of all the tension you feel in your shoulder and arm."

After a brief period of coaxing, the man's arm finally dropped to his side easily.

"If you want to understand what I have demonstrated here, the best thing to do is take a hatha yoga class. There are teachers here, and he pointed to people in the room. Mary Beth was among those pointed out.

"This knowledge of your body will benefit your meditation."

There were interesting things I discovered about the swami that didn't quite make sense. This man, reputed to be a complete master of yoga science, someone who had been a *Shankaracharya,* a sort of pope for Hindus, had also studied Shaolin Kung Fu.

His master had sent him to Tibet to study with a blind kung fu master. Intrigued by this, I didn't feel too silly when I thought about my attempts at finding a "true" teacher in a couple of men who taught martial arts. To that point, I'd thought only that martial arts training was a useful approach to meditation, even though I hadn't had much luck with martial arts teachers. I had started a karate class at my first active-duty station in the service. It had been so convenient, a little dojo right across the street from the base.

In Indianapolis, the karate master I found was a third-degree black belt in his martial art style. After taking classes with him for some months, the instructor came to us with a proposition.

"I am going to be taking payment for classes in a different way," he said. "If people have the money, they can pay for a year's instruction and get a discount on the year. What do you think?"

This was a great idea. I was going to classes at the university, I had my GI benefits, I was paying room and board at home, and I had just started a new job that one of my old college GI friends had helped me get. All the money I had, part of which I was socking away for something, yet unknown, I could use to pay for the instruction.

I paid the fees, and at the turn of the year, I showed up for my regular classes. I hadn't missed many classes, and I'd even won a trophy or two at local karate competitions for *kata,* demonstrations of form. I was continually looking beyond the veneer of technique to find the spiritual meaning behind all these roundhouse kicks and shouts of *keeeyaaa.*

The dojo was located in a small strip along a busy, north side street. One Saturday morning the parking lot seemed a bit empty, as I pulled my karate uniform out of the back of the car and walked to the front of the building. Things appeared dark inside. I looked at my watch and no, I was actually a bit late. I pressed the lever on the door and it didn't budge. Locked.

I knocked on the door, expecting to see *sensei* come from the back and let me in. The front part of the dojo where there were usually shelves with a few books and other things was gone. *Closed, how could it be closed, I had just paid my fees for a year's worth of instruction.* I was dumbstruck.

I fed on the ideas of the *Kung Fu* TV series. There was something in that series that touched me, that kept a spark alive in me. The images of David Carradine's character, Caine, interacting with a mythical, blind kung fu master fascinated me.

I didn't know how much of the series was Hollywood, but there the Shaolin monk got genuine instruction from old masters on a daily basis. They received instruction that combined martial arts with the beauty of the ideas that I read in a little book I treasured. The training was more about emotional maturity and mental balance than kicking three men in the face and breaking stones. Was it possible to get such profound instruction? The people I met certainly weren't the caliber of people who trained Caine. Did those kind of people really exist?

My friends chided me about my renegade karate *sensei* episode with the old adage, "A fool and his money are soon parted." I kept searching. I talked to martial artists in all the different styles.

An aikido black belt said, "I'm third degree and I have studied with the all the highest-ranking black belts in my tradition."

"Do you know about the spiritual aspects of the tradition?" I asked respectfully. "I have read the founders book, and there is a deep and practical spiritual aspect to aikido."

"I know all the techniques, but there is nothing spiritual that I have been taught. I don't think anybody knows this."

How could that be?

I kept asking questions and trying out teachers. The free local activities publications, the ones that all major cities have that tell about fitness, special events, and the like, advertised an introductory class in tai chi.

I listened to Jerry, the instructor, on the first night of the free class.

"Tai chi is one of the triad of Chinese internal martial arts. It is known as the Grand Ultimate Pugilism." Jerry was a local man who had studied elsewhere.

"Tai chi is ultimately concerned with *chi,*" he went on, "the ultimate vital energy in the body, the energy that pervades the entire universe." I didn't quite know what this *chi* was, but what he said stirred something in me.

I threw myself into the practice of it and found out that another name for tai chi was Taoist yoga. A famous grand master, Cheng Man Cheng, was once asked about the difference between yoga and tai chi.

Master Cheng is reported to have said, "With tai chi, if someone takes your cushion from you, you can take it back." Coming from an internal martial artist who supposedly could absorb or evade the punches of the most adept boxers, it was intriguing at the time to what remained of my military-trained mind.

Jerry, an artist and a gentle soul, let me hang around him for a while gleaning as much as I could from him about tai chi. I began my study with him at a Shotokan karate dojo where our tai chi class shared the space and sparred with these hard style karate practitioners. When the lease ran out at the dojo, he allowed me into his home, where he worked with me one on one.

"Jerry, when I move so slowly with the breath, I feel something surging in my hands. It's the same feeling that you get when you have done heavy exercise and your fingers feel like they are larger than they really are because of the blood flow."

"That's a sign that you have the *chi* moving in your body. Are you sure this is your experience?"

"Yep, I'm sure."

"You're doing well with what you've learned, Charles."

Was *chi* really this simple? I didn't think that I had any special talent for this work, but I sure had the desire to understand it. The more I read about it and tried to understand its nature, the more I glimpsed the healing power of *chi*. I could cultivate and move the *chi* without the physical movements—it really had nothing to do with martial arts at all, it was all something internal. *Chi* was the foundation of acupuncture. Beyond that, it had spiritual implications, implications that I didn't yet understand, but I learned as much as I could before there was a startling change.

I had continued my mediation practice and the Taoist yoga was a good prelude to sitting. Every morning at 5:00 a.m., I would stretch, do my short set, take a shower, and go to my meditation seat. I sat in front of a mirror so that I could see if my posture was correct and if it changed after sitting for twenty or thirty minutes. I did this because of the information about proper posture I'd gotten from pictures I'd seen in meditation and tai chi books, books I'd searched high and low for in new and used bookstores around Indianapolis.

Then it came. "Charles, you should know that tai chi is satanic."

"Oh, come on now, Jerry. What's happened to you? How could understanding yourself be satanic?"

He had recently joined a church with his new wife. He was going to what were new places for him, but for me, places I had already been, and come away disappointed.

"One of the most amazing things known to man, directly linked to evolving human consciousness, and it's now satanic?" I said the very words I'd heard him say more than once.

"It's satanic and I'm never teaching this again . . . "

Considering all this, it seemed a good idea to consider where I might formally study the physical exercise that the swami had talked about. Neither Mary Beth nor the deli existed anymore, they had disappeared around the time of that eventful evening with the swami. It was almost as though they had only existed to set me up for that night. The place where she taught was also the place that had sponsored the swami. It was at this little center, the Himalayan Institute, that I began the study of hatha yoga, the physical culture aspect of yoga. I was more than a bit skeptical when I arrived for my first class.

The practice room's walls were paneled and the floor was covered with brown flowered carpet. That first night, half-dozen women sat around the floor waiting for the teacher to come in. I was waiting for some other men to show up—in 1979. When the instructor showed up, I introduced myself. Rose was a soft-spoken, dark-haired, kind woman, some ten years or so my elder. I found out she was an initiate of the swami, whatever that meant. All sorts of things ran through my mind about these yoga classes.

"So ladies, where are all the guys?" The ladies chuckled and looked at me as if I were from outer space.

"There aren't any guys who come to this class," one lady spoke up.

"Oh, so they come to other classes at other times?" All the ladies chuckled again as Rose asked the class to lay in *shavasana,* the corpse pose. I had been stretching in my martial arts classes, but poses like the triangle *(uthitta trikonasana)* and revolving triangle *(parivritti trikonasana)* were challenging. I didn't know why. I truly enjoyed the sun salutations *(surya namaskar),* with its downward facing dog (*adhomukha svanasana*) and cobra (*bujangasan*a) poses. Funny names, but many of them, when translated, reminded me of names given to martial arts positions, positions often associated with animals and their particular qualities, often their ferocity. The yoga poses were a bit different even though there were poses like the warrior (*virabhadrasana),* an aggressive-sounding, demanding pose among the repertoire of poses. Names like that made me feel less out of place, although the emphasis in all the classes was on peace.

I attended a couple of eight-week classes, learning the secret about relaxation that the swami had presented on that first night, before coming to an insight. The attendance in yoga class was pretty much like the attendance in church. The pews in church, and the classes in yoga, were filled with women. Looking around the room of yoga students in my class, I couldn't help but make the comparison to one of the enigmas of my youth. I was, more often than not, the only man in the yoga class.

The swami who spoke to us that night in the bank conference

room didn't say anything about hatha yoga being only for women. As far as I could tell, he was the man's man. In his cave monastery, there were only men. What did the essence of yoga have to do with gender anyway? What did the essence of church have to do with gender? There was something in both places that transcended gender. How very mundane that awareness was to me.

CHAPTER FOUR

Forlorned Dreaming

Aside from the influence of having a twin sister, my mother's strength and social activism colored my perception of the world, and played a subtle role in how I found myself in that basement. Things that I took for granted in my neighborhood came from my mother's hard work and perseverance. The paved street in front of the house that had dirt paths along it for walking got sidewalks.

Every home on our side of the street along the block had a bridge that crossed the open ditch, a ditch you might expect to see in some underdeveloped country. The contamination from a local plant eventually prevented us from catching crawdads or playing in the water. From seeing that sewers were put in to seeing to it that the dust bowls where I played basketball were leveled and black-topped, my mother played in the neighborhood, a role whose significance I really didn't understand.

"Charles Buford, come here and look at this," my mother said to me as we walked back to the little room she and dad had added on to our side of the double.

"What do you want me to see, Momma?"

There on the wall hung a plaque, an award she'd received from the governor. The plaque read "Sagamore of the Wabash."

"Do you want to know what it means?"

"No, ma'am, I don't really"

I'd never heard of this thing, but it seemed important, if only to her. Some of the people in the political circles she ran in irritated me. They always mispronounced her name. It was Al–ene, not A–lene. Here on the wall was something else, though.

Momma said, "The early tribes of Indiana used the term "sagamore" to describe a lesser chief, someone who the chief consulted for advice."

"So that's what the governor thinks of you, huh?" I chuckled. I found out that it was, at the time, the highest award the state of Indiana gives a civilian. This unassuming little woman had received an award whose prior recipients included presidents, ambassadors, artists, and astronauts. My mother was a lot more than just a little black lady who wore fine hats to church. There was something else about Momma, though, something uncommon, and in the early days of my life, she let me in on it, something that would affect the rest of my life. She revealed a mystery in a story told to my twin sister and me.

In a quiet moment amid all her household and community work, Momma astonished us with a story about her life before we had been born. It was a story about a man named John Taylor. This all came about from my meddling in a dresser drawer where I found a string tie, a tie like the old cowboys, the Lone Ranger and Gene Autry, wore.

I really liked this tie. The string was a blend of gold and black interwoven fibers with shiny silver metal tips to keep the ends from fraying. A silver metal clasp held the strings together, and on the silver clasp in a black background were letters.

The letters on the face of the clasp read JT. I secretly wore it to school, and one day, home from school, the thought came: *What do the letters, JT, stand for?*

I asked Neenee what she thought, "Maybe it stands for somebody's name."

I never associated the letters with anyone's name. We both approached our mother.

"Momma, what does the JT on this tie stand for?"

There was a pause and a puzzled expression on momma's face. It was that look she gave us when she didn't know just how to explain something.

"JT stands for John Taylor, my first husband."

First husband, what did she mean first husband? Hadn't she always, since the beginning of time, been married to my daddy? Neenee and I both listened in childhood bewilderment.

"I was nineteen when I married John. He was killed in a car accident."

We could hear the deep sadness in Momma's voice.

"I was so heartbroken by his death that for a while I considered entering a convent. After a long time, I started to feel like I could live in the world and be happy again."

Convent? More intriguing than the mystery of a convent was the extraordinary love story she told us. I let the mysterious word pass.

"When I started dating again, something special happened. Whenever a young man asked me out, my dear John would appear."

My sister and I sat with ever-widening eyes listening to this story. "Momma, what do you mean, he would appear"?

"It was always near the end of the date when I was being taken back home, as we were walking up to the door. Every time I'd have a date, John would appear and motion that this man was not the person for me."

My mind raced.

Momma is joking with us, right? How is it possible? How could a dead man show up on a date? But, she wouldn't tell us a lie would she, a lie with so much pain attached to it? This wasn't like Santa Claus was it?

No! What she was saying was something that really happened. We could see it in her eyes.

"John kept coming and interrupting my dates until I met your father. When I met your daddy, John appeared one last time, smiled, and motioned to me that this was the right guy, and that I need look no farther."

In the short time it took her to tell us this story, we had completely empathized with our mother's painful loss and the comfort she found in John's loving assistance. It was almost as if he were our father, our little minds unable to discern a difference. It was comforting to know that someone, something, behind the scenes, was looking out for my Momma's happiness in this world. My sister and I were both saddened when she told us that he'd never again returned.

Decades later, as I tried to flesh out the meaning behind this story, I wondered if it was possible that John's love and concern for my mom had moved him to straddle the barrier between life and death. So many times, I disappointed my mom doing foolish things, and it was in those moments that I wondered if she ever had second thoughts about revealing such a deep and intimate secret to such a foolish boy? The dirty cowboy boots, on the wrong feet, at church, or the bathroom shower curtains that I shredded out of wonder at the sharpness of a double-edged razor. I was sure the trouble I had caused her would have made her second guess her decision if she had only known. Contradictions beyond my understanding made it easy for me to accept my mother's story and hard to accept some of the things I was taught about religion; and then there was the taunting of neighborhood boys.

One day I was roughhousing with boys in the park and one asked, "What do you get out of church? We see you going there all the time."

"Well . . . "

"You only go to church 'cause your momma makes you go."

"That's not true." I questioned my words while I was saying them. Although it was true that Momma was the one who advocated our going to church, Dad always supported the idea.

Another boy spoke up, "My daddy said that church is what women use to try to break the spirit of a man. Church makes you a sissy."

I understood what they were implying, but I didn't understand if they were right.

"Un-uhhh, there are men in church."

"Yea, but those men are sissies. The woman runs that house."

Even though they didn't know it, the boys who taunted me had been fed on the propaganda of women's inferiority. My experience with my twin had made me see that this was all wrong, but dare I say this out loud?

The Baptist church's point of view of other sects, denominations, and religions added to the confusion. I was taught that Islam, Judaism, and Catholicism were all innately evil. Buddhism or Hinduism didn't have a presence in the surrounding neighborhood, only on the world scene, but they were evil, too. Jews, Muslims, Catholics, Buddhist, and Hindus were all going to hell because they didn't "believe" as Baptists did. The Jewish people were going to hell because they killed Jesus. The Muslims were going to hell because they didn't have the proper understanding of Jesus. The Catholics were just going to hell because they started it all and supposedly lost sight of the goal by introducing the worship of God's mother, among other things. The Buddhists didn't believe in God, and the Hindus had too many. The misconceptions were astounding, and all who attended Sunday School, as I did, were conditioned to accept them without question.

There were things I learned that were more painful and more immediate than going or not going to heaven. These things came from the world outside my backyard, and just beyond the boundaries of my small neighborhood. The confusion created in church was not nearly as painful as the reality in the larger world.

The overall well-being of our family was on the rock that was my dad, who, as any good dad does, taught me important life lessons. When I was nine or ten, he took me along to his part-time job cleaning banks. He hustled up these extra jobs to make sure that we had all that we needed in life. What I learned riding along with him and working at those part time jobs was priceless.

"Son, you want to learn how to approach things systematically. Look at a space and analyze how you want to approach cleaning it. Daddy stood me by the door and went about with his dust mop, getting every nook and cranny of the office space, ending up with a nice pile right in front of me. His movements were effortless, like those of the Zen archers I would read about who effortlessly hit bull's-eyes even in the dark. Their movements were as natural as a drop of water falling from a leaf after a rain. He made the mundane work an art with his understanding of systematically approaching a job.

"Doing it one way might cause you to repeat steps or retrace ground you've already covered, wasting your time and your effort," he said.

"I don't get it, daddy."

"Doing things in a systematic way saves time. It gets the best results because you don't miss anything."

This lesson about being thorough and systematic was one already learned when I heard the same from my spiritual teacher when it came to yoga.

When dad was a teenager, he had gone off to serve his country in the Navy during World War II. He never told me about any fights he had growing up, and I knew that he wasn't a violent person, but he did think it useful for me to learn boxing. He'd done some boxing in the Navy. Knowing how to box proved to be of great value in the neighborhood streets. Some people considered it violence, but in the hands of an activist like Muhammad Ali, it was an art.

"Son, if you don't look like you know what you're doing in the neighborhood, then you might be at risk. Keep your dukes up."

I stood there with my guard up as my dad shot little slap boxing jabs at me. As I got older and stronger, Dad stopped challenging me to put my dukes up, because I grew to have faster hand speed than he did. My dad's prompting me to look like I knew what I was doing came in handy when I was challenged a time or two on the streets.

At least, that was his experience in life. The neighborhood changed a lot in his lifetime. Growing up, I found that prowess on the basketball court was important—this prowess translated into respect on the street. Like everywhere else in the U.S., jocks got the glory and the girls.

My dad bolstered my young mind against the neighborhood boys' taunts about going to church. He was no religious scholar, but his simple words, "Don't ever forget your spiritual training," served me well.

Often, through great turmoil, he provided the bedrock for all the good things that happened in my childhood. Dad hardly ever missed a day of work at a factory job where he often came in direct contact with coworkers who were members of the Ku Klux Klan. The hatred they rained on him came in subtle and overt ways. My father tried to explain the KKK to me.

One evening when I was about thirteen years old, while I passed through the living room where my dad sat watching his evening news program, he stopped me.

"Charlie, stop here. Watch this. It's important," he said. "This is something you should know about."

I hated the news; cartoons and comedies were the only shows worth watching on TV.

"This evening, in our exposé, we will look into the murky world of the Ku Klux Klan," said the news correspondent.

These were the people my dad wanted me to know something about, but I didn't know why. I found out that I didn't want to know what I learned, but there was no escaping it. There, before my eyes, were pictures of the KKK coming out of a church in an orderly procession. The interviewer asked one man, "What do you teach your children?"

A man sitting with his two children, both younger than me, directed them to speak up. "Boys, now what've I taught you?"

The youngest one spoke up, "I hate Niggers and Jews."

I was simultaneously terrified and grief stricken at the child's words.

What had I done to these people that they, not knowing me, would call me or members of my family that name, and why would they hate me?

My dad didn't seem mortified at all at what I had just witnessed. He said to me, wisely, "Remember, not everyone in this world is going to like you."

I didn't want everyone to like me, but I had no enemies. There was no reason for these people to hate me was there?

At thirteen, after viewing the news special on the KKK that dad forced me to watch, I went through newspaper articles in the public library archives. They revealed images of lynchings, not fifty miles away from where I lived, and KKK parades in the nation's capital. I was frightened and angered to see that movies were made like *The Birth of a Nation,* movies that glorified the role of the KKK and its goal of protecting American society against the scourge of the black male child.

My young mind convulsed in turmoil at the self-destructive thought:

You don't want to be one of those black male children. But . . . I am—a black . . . male . . . child.

A horrible disconnect established itself and played out in my mind during the social unrest that was happening all around me.

I asked my dad, "What'd these people do that policemen are setting dogs on them?" These people looked like me. I tried the best I could to justify what I saw. I tried to reconcile my fear with being at peace with myself and the world—it never happened.

"They must have done something pretty bad for the police to treat them this way, didn't they Daddy?"

"All they've done is stand up for human kindness and dignity," Dad said.

Aside from their best efforts, my parents were, in a sense, powerless. They unknowingly witnessed the mind of their child be tainted, be contaminated, by fear. How could they ever protect me from that? There was no further discussion. There were no rational answers for questions like this in my community. It was a source of great sadness, fear, and anger.

No one ever spoke aloud about the conditions because the unspoken response from the larger world seemed to be, "We don't want to hear that. If you lift your voice and speak of your rights as a human being, you are not keeping to your place. Lifting your voice will destroy our society. Aren't you ashamed of yourself?"

My sadness and confusion grew. Fear subtly shaped everything. Fleeting was the sense of everyone, everything being from one source. There were no means to sustain this sense. It had just been a folly of youth. Over time, the fear, concealed by anger, led to forgetting. Then it was time to go to high school.

My mom and dad had gone to the only schools allowed for them to attend, colored schools, but 1965 saw my sister and me enrolled in an integrated high school. Here, for the first time, I heard the little jokes and rhymes that floated around the larger culture, the culture outside my tiny neighborhood, about "those" black folk. Two white classmates spoke to each other by the lockers in the main hallway, unaware of my presence.

"What did you say to him, Jeff?" They snickered as they talked with each other.

"I told this colored kid, here are the rules: If you're brown, come around, if you're black, stay back!" They both laughed as they looked up from their joke and saw me. The lockers closed, and the boys made their way to their next class.

I'd been blessed, I thought, to be assigned to accelerated classes. Classes for kids who were on the fast track for college and who had exceptional grades coming into high school. At the time, I had no understanding of the special nature of the classes I was assigned to, I was just going to school. By the end of four years, I was president of the orchestra, and played in the pit orchestra and jazz band for special school functions. I was just as good at basketball, but the music took precedence. Here, as in church, music was my way to soar above the contradictions and injustice in the world. Music let my thinking mind retire, and emotion to come forward. But it was more than that. Music, when done well, left me with this oceanic feeling of peace and harmony that united all and excluded nothing. This was an experience I couldn't explain, but it was oh, so real, but only within the confines of music, or so I trained myself.

On the high school basketball court, I was more likely to run into those guys with the little jokes to tell that were always at my expense. The punch line always involved the stupid or inept "colored" man. With music, I was always above the fray, especially when the riots between white children and black children happened in high school. I happened to be one of the student leaders the school administration called upon to speak to the student body to help quell such disturbances. I felt that since I was among the elite in high school they, the elite, would certainly be above the misconceptions of racial prejudice.

My naiveté regarding racial intolerance among the elite was no more telling than what happened one day after a few of us wrote and presented a one-act comedy. Every year our high school presented an evening of one-act comedies. Our cast was composed of black and white friends and family members. In my heart of hearts, beneath this anger/hidden fear, I held on to the truth that our fictional creation, the harmony of our combined cast, could be a reality. This was not unlike the dream of Dr. Martin Luther King Jr. The play was one of the firsts for black children at the high school. I would find this moniker of "first" to be a burden.

We presented a comic parody of the musical *Showboat,* with our mixed cast playing all the roles. The original musical was set during the time of riverboats, and before the emancipation of slaves. During one provocative scene, a cast member walked slowly and menacingly across the stage dressed as a Klansman. When the sordid figure got to the middle of the stage, the actor removed his hood. Beneath it was a black male child.

"Fooled ya', didn't I!"

The auditorium became eerily silent. There was no laughter, no audible sound of shock, just stone, cold silence. I was to be confronted with the repercussions of our one act comedy a few days after the play. In physics class, a redheaded boy pulled me to the side.

The boy said, "Don't you know that we can come into your neighborhood and wipe out your entire family and get out without anybody ever knowing it?"

I can't say that I saw hatred in the boy's face, but he did have a contemptible expression. I'd seen his look on the faces of thugs on the basketball courts in my neighborhood, an expression that boasted prowess, but was rarely backed up with true skills on the court. I was quite used to this look.

This boy couldn't possibly mean what he was saying. Nobody would have the nerve to say this out loud, to my face.

He didn't back down. We stared at each other eye to eye for

some time, and then he walked away. My dad had tried to educate
me about such things more than once. Idealistic children either
don't listen or don't understand. He had worked at that Chrysler
plant all of my life, around grown men who treated him like this.

When I responded to the interest that a little white girl had in
me, he warned me.

"What are you doing, son, with this white girl?"

"I'm not doing anything Daddy. She just said that she had a
dream about me and we got to talking. She's nice."

"You shouldn't pay attention to such things. This will cause
trouble for you."

I sat there listening to my dad. I couldn't figure out if his words
were a warning or words of bias. Either way I was saddened. He
was trying his best to protect me from the type of danger that this
boy standing in front of me posed. I never reported the incident to
the teachers or to my family. The concealment of such things was
an everyday occurrence in my community. Who was really going
to protect me from such real or threatened violence? Who? I was
wary from that point on, as I stood alone at bus stops near the
school after late music rehearsals. I was sure I could handle myself
against one thug, but not so sure about a gang of thugs, or adults
with tire irons.

The light of hope amid all this turmoil in high school was the
efforts of Dr. Martin Luther King Jr. What I heard in the words of
his "Dream" was bigger than black or white; it had something to
do with what I still held on to secretly as true.

"…But it really doesn't matter with me now, because I've been
to the mountaintop. And I don't mind. Like anybody, I would
like to live a long life – longevity has its place. But I'm not concerned about that now…I've looked over, and I've seen the Promised Land…

I'm not fearing any man. Mine eyes have seen the glory of the
coming of the Lord."

Prophetic words of Dr. King on a night in 1968, harbinger of a
day when peaceful intentions in the wilderness of human violence
would be assassinated.

A light further dimmed inside me, the light of the dream had been assassinated. The only person who seemed to know the way was gone. I didn't know how he came about what he knew, but I knew his dream and my yearning, at the core, had something in common.

By seventeen, the wound of my separateness was completely opened. The pristine nature of my being—lost. Like everyone else now, I seemed destined to wander the bright streets and side streets of this world looking for a way to be at peace with myself, stranded with the idea that oneness was . . .

CHAPTER FIVE

Free Your Mind

By the time all these events had transpired in high school, I had done everything you could do in the church, everything except deliver a sermon. I was never attracted to the pulpit. I was interested in something more, some inexplicable other.

This unknowingly led to a defining conversation with my mother. My mind in turmoil, I found myself with my mother as she looked out the window above the kitchen sink. She'd told me many times that she'd gotten many insights while washing dishes looking out that window. It was almost theatre that our conversation took place there.

"Momma, I'm not going to go to church anymore."

She had that concerned expression on her face that you just never really wanted to see on your momma's face, but I continued.

"Church just doesn't make any sense. There's all these contradictions."

She continued to listen knowingly, the look of consternation softening around the edges.

She said softly, "Many a boy like you has lost his way in those streets out there."

Losing your way in the surrounding neighborhood often meant a life of crime, or getting a girl pregnant and working in some low-wage job trying to make ends meet. I don't really know how I escaped the tragedy of this. The conversation with Momma continued.

"You know, Momma, you trying to help me with this problem is like you trying to help me with trigonometry. Since you don't know the rules of trig, you can't help me get past this point."

My remarks were a stunning but accurate summation of my condition that just rolled off my lips. I expected a thunderous response, but there was none. The look in her eyes was a look of helpless compassion. She let me walk away without any other words, no doubt holding back every motherly instinct she had.

With this confusion and in spite of it, I pressed on. So began my first days in college. The first people I met in college in the fall of 1969 immediately began to shape my future choices. They were veterans, black GIs, recently returned from the jungles of Vietnam, and elsewhere, who were getting college degrees paid for with the GI bill. We all attended the local extension of Purdue University.

"Vietnam was beautiful, brother, and terrifying all at the same time."

These were the words of one GI friend, Peter, nearly killed in action, and receiving permanent disability for service related injuries. He showed me pictures of himself sitting in a wheelchair somewhere in 'Nam. A bullet had ripped through his neck and face and left him with a scar that was just a minor distraction when you talked to this vibrant, intelligent black veteran.

Then there was Chuck. Chuck was a reddish-brown-skinned brother with hair to match, and, if he hadn't been married, he would have been one to play havoc with the hearts of the ladies. I wondered if he did anyway. He was a smooth talking, lean, good-looking brother whose face was set off by a distinctive Fu Manchu. And then there was the one marine who simply went by the name we gave him, Sinister McNasty.

"So, what do you have to do to get the GI bill?" I asked these guys, just out of curiosity.

"All you have to do is two years of service, and be honorably discharged," was the quick reply from Peter.

"Nope, that's just for Army, Marine Corps is four," chimed in McNasty.

A furious game of bid whist, the card game of choice, was going on around a large round table in the spacious student lounge. The dimly lit lounge was filled with fake leather couches with little, knee-high square tables situated around them. The room acted as a study area at the couches or a bid whist game room for us in the middle.

"The bid is four to you, Crenshaw."

"Pass," I said, wondering what it was about these men that drew me to them. These guys were so different from the average guy in the neighborhood. These men were on a mission to finish their education. There were no questions in their mind about it, and it seemed that the military had something to do with it. I didn't know why it made a difference, but it did.

"Did you brothers enlist in the service?"

"Nope!" came the reply from two of the guys, almost in unison. Peter said, "Chuck and I were both drafted."

Most of the GIs I met had been drafted, and they were all full of knowledge about the world, some I could get on any street corner in the neighborhood, but some I couldn't.

"What was the most interesting thing that you learned in the service?" There had to be some special knowledge that they had.

"Ah, man, it was great to travel and see how other people in the world live," McNasty said.

Chuck said, "L'il brother, it was great to see all the different kinds of women around the world." It was obvious what his primary interest had been, and being young and burning, as they say, his remarks stirred things up.

"The people in places like Viet Nam practice Buddhism."

Buddhism, that somehow struck a nerve. It stirred something in me related to my childhood. I was eighteen. I'd seen images of the Buddha, and heard about Buddhism on TV, monks were immolating themselves in protest of the war. Real information about Buddhism or Buddhist practices wasn't the kind of thing that floated around the streets of my neighborhood.

"Hey, Chuck, isn't that the same thing that the Beatles do?"

"No, man. You got things all mixed up," he said. The Beatles don't have anything to do with Buddhism per se."

The men chuckled at my mistake.

McNasty grunted, "Man, the only beetles we saw in the jungles of 'Nam were crawling on the ground."

"The Beatles sing about the stuff of this Maharishi dude," said Peter. "Coltrane and the Parliament Funkadelics are into that kind of stuff too."

"What do you mean," I asked, "Why would you say the Funkadelics knew anything about Buddhism?"

"Naw, not Buddhism, at least I don't think, but the lyrics to their songs have a message somewhat akin to what the Beatles and Coltrane were into."

"Yeah, yeah," chimed in Chuck, "Free your mind and your ass will follow, the kingdom of heaven is within. That's not quite your Sunday School hymn lyric, now is it?" Everyone laughed, but my laugh was uneasy. Those words meant something to me. Free your mind . . . the kingdom of heaven is within.

Parliament Funkadelics. I'd more than seen the name and heard their music. About the same time I started college, some of my high school music friends started a band, and with them I began an ill-fated career as an R&B musician. The memory of being lifted out of myself through the music of the great masters in high school orchestra, or the music in church, is what fueled this desire for R&B superstardom.

Dressing the part, I wore the clothes of people like Sly, of Sly and the Family Stone, and Jimi Hendrix. I practiced hard to find the way to enlightenment through music. Coltrane was turning out *A Love Supreme*, reaching for something I knew I could find, if I only knew the way through music.

The Fabulous Expressions Show Band and Review was our name. We offered a show with solo singers as well as a trio; we had a lot of people to pay. There were seven of us. Kevin was the star vocalist. Bobbie played trumpet and was Kevin's second on vocals, Clint finished up the trio and also played bongos and congas. Rocky played drums, PC on keyboards, KW on reeds—tenor sax and flute, and I was the bass man. In our time, we were good enough to open for a few name acts like the Delfonics and the Originals, names that

R&B aficionados would recognize. The road to freeing my mind met with a serious detour early one morning after a long weekend with the band.

Looking at my watch, it was 4:50 a.m. The weekend had been a joy. We had been the warm-up band for the Originals at a venue in Evansville, Indiana. What more could a kid want than to be playing music at a show with one of the hottest R&B acts of the day?

I opened the back door to our house and stepped quietly in. The lights were out, but I knew Dad would be getting up soon to go to work. I made my way past my parents' bedroom and into the middle bedroom where I slept. As I crawled into bed, dad's alarm clock went off. He got out of bed, certain to have heard me come in, put the light on, and came to my room.

He's just checking to see that I'm in. It's good to be home, this sleeping in the car stuff and the dinky hotels wasn't much fun. I was eventually going to find nirvana, though, so it had to be worth it.

"Boy, where you been?"

Excited, I said, "I was playing a gig with the band. We went to Owensboro and . . . "

"What do you mean you went playin' with the band? You didn't tell your momma (code for I was worried about you) where you were going. You didn't call. You didn't tell us anything about the last two days. Are you crazy? If you're going to do this kind of thing, you can just get your stuff together and move out."

I didn't know what to say. I wasn't prepared for this.

"Pop, to me playing in the band was like playing in the high school orchestra or jazz band. You don't really need to make a big fuss about it, everything is properly chaperoned and all." This was as near to a lie as I wanted to get.

"I don't wanna hear that nonsense," and he stormed down the stairs to prepare for work. I knew not to follow him. He went away that morning more disturbed with me than I'd ever seen him. After he left for work, I sought solace from my mother.

"Momma, does he really mean that I have to get out? Where will I go? I didn't mean to do anything wrong."

"Your father is concerned that you are going to run into problems."

"What kind of problems could I have that he'd threaten to throw me out? I don't understand."

"Honey, this isn't like the high school orchestra or jazz band. There are dangers."

"What kind of dangers?"

I hadn't mentioned any dangers, like the car that careened off our rear end in Cincinnati, on the way to a gig on a steamboat. When Dad came home, Momma talked to him and I was saved from, what seemed to me, a new life with my luggage at the shelter house in the park. Sitting on my anger at what I considered my father's lack of understanding and trust in me, I listened to the reasoning behind his actions.

"Charlie, I watched the jazz musicians when I was younger. They were always stoned half out of their minds. They were wasted on heroin and other things."

"Heroin? Daddy, I don't do drugs." But I was also naïve. "Coltrane said music is the spiritual expression of what I am—my faith, my knowledge, my being," a quote I'd read, but I didn't know how to explain what I meant to my dad. He was not privy to my sense of wonder at the unity I saw in everything. I kept this part of myself hidden from even him.

"Son, did you know that Coltrane was a heroin addict?"

"Naw, not Coltrane, he was all about this spiritual thing, like I am. Don't you see?"

"You look into this a bit further, and you let me know what you find out."

These last words should have been the words of our loving interaction, but in the heat of the moment, they weren't. After a little thought, and some research, I begrudgingly resigned myself to just being a serious student, and not a serious student slash bass player slash R&B superstar. This was the first time I felt that I might have made a mistake passing up the partial music scholarship I'd been offered. I followed my head, going for a computer technology degree, instead of my heart. I'd learn the consequences of not listening to my heart.

Music was a catalyst that supported my urge for transcendence, a transcendence whose source I didn't know. Dad's concern was legitimate. I was angry with him for forcing me to make a decision.

Back at school, which was going on right alongside my show-biz escapades, I'd started down the road that my mother feared I would. I found myself in a lust-filled relationship with a female classmate, a relationship that I was too immature to handle, a further distraction from schoolwork, and something that confounded the search for transcendence. Child of the sixties, free love, drugs, I pondered if sex was truly a way to transcendence any more or less than drugs? Overwhelmed by issues that needed resolution, I floundered in school. The conversations with those GIs around the card table made an impact on me.

"Hey, Henry, man, I need to take a break. I'm not applying myself here. Something is all wrong."

"What are you thinking? You know that they just ordered an escalation for Vietnam, right?"

"Yeah, man, I know. They pulled my number, so if I am not in school, then I'm drafted. I know enough from you brothers that Vietnam is not the place to go."

"So, what are you going to do?"

"I don't' know."

I decided to talk to my dad. If nothing else, he was practical. I had enough faith in him to consider that he wouldn't knowingly steer me wrong, and after all, he was also a veteran.

"Dad, I think I need to take a break from school." My father worked hard at the Chrysler factory to pay for two college educations at the local extensions. Factory wages, UAW or not, did not provide enough resources for two children in school at once.

"Charlie, you know what happens to young men from the neighborhood who aren't in school."

"Yeah, I know. You know the brothers from school, most of them have been to 'Nam."

"Is that what you wanna do, go to Vietnam?"

"No, sir. I just know that I need a pause to clear my head or something . . . something to get back on track." It was now 1971. Little did I really know all the forces that were impelling me to seek this change.

"Pop, what I do know is that right now I'm wasting your hard-earned money. I have to do something." He was happy with my maturity about his sacrifice, but he was as equally disheartened about my idea of leaving school, as my mother had been about my leaving church.

Destiny was calling, and I didn't know it, and unbeknownst to anyone I'd made an appointment with the Navy recruiter just so I'd know all my options.

"What are you looking for young man?" asked the Navy recruiter. The first class petty officer was in his dress blues, with the perfectly tied square knot in his hand-rolled black scarf, that was placed strategically around the white striped collar of his uniform. There were four gold stripes running diagonally on the forearm of his sleeve. The darkly furnished office was a small place, with two desks, one for him and one for the other recruiter.

"I understand that if I enlist, I can get the GI bill, is that right? Uncle Sam will pay for my education?"

"You have to enlist for four years, and there is a two-year inactive reserve requirement," came the recruiters reply.

"Four years? The GIs at school said you only needed to do two years." The brothers around the bid whist table had been adamant about only spending two years in the service. What this recruiter said made no sense.

"Your friends were drafted, right?"

"Well, yeah, but what's that got to do with it?"

"The Navy doesn't draft, and we don't have a two-year enlistment program. There are only four-year and six-year enlistments."

Woah! Six years or even four years, that's a long time to be away from home.

An all-too-familiar scene from my childhood flashed before me.

"Now, you children behave yourselves, and don't give Granny any problems. All right?" These were Momma's words to my sister and me as my parents walked down the stairs of my maternal grandmother's public housing apartment, and toward the door to head back to Indianapolis. Visiting with our grandmother was always an extraordinary time, because she was truly the doting grandmother, and we loved her for that. There was only one problem.

As soon as my parents hit the door, I began to wail. I cried, and I had no reason for why I was crying. There was this terrible pain in my heart that I just couldn't account for it. It was as though I was being abandoned.

"What's the matter with you Channa?" Neenee said. I had no answer for her only more tears. This went on for days.

How am I going to handle four years away from home if I couldn't handle three weeks away from my parents with my sister right next to me?

The recruiter said, "Well, young man what d'ya think?" I was back from my mental flight.

"Well . . . ?"

"Oh yeah, there is one more thing that I can tell you. For your two years of college, you'll get two pay grades at the end of boot camp. You'll be a seaman first class rather than a seaman recruit."

I would get more money for college than I thought. I would get money for having some college, and enough money to finish my undergrad and more with the GI Bill.

I thought the Navy's deal over and without confiding in anyone else, I enlisted.

"Son, you're not gonna like the service," my dad said as he, my mother, and my sisters all gathered in Momma's little kitchen, between the washer, the stove and the counters. He knew my temperament, and he wondered how I was going to make it in the military.

Cocksure of myself I said, "Yeah, but I'm nineteen, and I've already signed the papers. There's no turning back now."

My dad was puzzled by my enlistment.

"Do you know what that means?"

"Pop, I know my number for the draft has already been pulled. If I had officially stayed out for a semester, they would have drafted me and sent me to 'Nam to kill people."

As I saw it, I was the perfect candidate for inclusion in the illusion called war. There was no other way out. Little did I know how right I was.

"School could've kept you safe if you had only put your shoulder to the wheel, but it's too late now." For the first time ever, I noticed a bit of sadness in my dad's voice. As a boy, my dad had sat me down and told me the most fascinating stories.

"You know, when you are out at sea, it is the most beautiful thing. Nothing but water as far as the eye can see in all directions. The air is fresh and clear. The full moon on the ocean is a wonderful thing to see. It sparkles in the water from the ship to the horizon. You can never see this sort of thing on land."

Innocently, my young imagination was filled with the beauty of the ocean, and stories of exotic ports. The other side of the story, the side I paid the least attention to, the side I that I overlooked, were his stories of sitting behind his forty-millimeter guns shooting at Japanese kamikaze planes, and stepping over dead bodies.

He would tell me, "At night, you could see where you were shooting because they had these tracer bullets. They emitted light so you could see where you were shooting."

I never registered the real stress and danger in his stories about combat, but his stories were just the kind of thing that could fill a young boy's mind with visions of heroic exploits, and not incline him toward the truth of death and war. For my dad, it was a statement of facts and not meant to fuel a young boy's foolish imagination.

CHAPTER SIX

Headed in an Eastern Direction

Barely twenty years old in January 1972, I was on my way to boot camp. I knew one thing. I didn't want to kill people. I'd been trained well, and a life not in school held no promise for me. One thing the Navy offered was structure. The military was my first real freedom from the influence of community, religion, and family.

"All right, you recruits line up by the bunks," the company commander barked.

"Atten-hut." I snapped to attention, as best I knew, as did most of the other recruits. The company commander gave us our first instructions in military protocol, and we practiced a bit.

I had enough natural discipline to be selected recruit company commander, thanks in part to having been a lieutenant in my grade school safety patrol. This meant that I was second in command to the chief petty officer, who was the real company commander. It was in the service that I found myself theoretically on par with every other man; the Uniform Code of Military Justice made sure of that.

Boot camp seemed an odd place for me to experience a sense of freedom, but it was there, for the first time, that I gave myself permission to attend a Catholic mass. The mass held in a large hall was officiated by a real priest, dressed in his vestments, doing everything in Latin. I looked around at the host of recruits from all the different companies and parroted their movements and responses as best I could. This exercise in freedom challenged my distorted view of Catholicism. Contrary to what I was taught, Baptists did believe the same basic things as Catholics, and prayed to the same god. Nine cold winter weeks flew by at Great Lakes Naval Training Center, and I was off to technical school and afterwards my first duty station.

Technical school was not the place to continue a serious inquiry into things spiritual. Out in the boonies, in a place called Bainbridge Maryland, I studied to be a radio communications–teletype specialist. I turned down the offers to trade six years of my life for training in electronics, computers, or going to nuke (nuclear power) school.

In tech school, I worked hard to graduate number one in my class, but was beat out by a rival from Notre Dame and a cowboy from Texas. Odd though it seemed, I chose my first duty station as Omaha Nebraska. An interesting decision, and one that reflected my attachment to home and an interest in a girl.

In Omaha, with one of my sailor friends, I often found myself in a trendy part of town that had a little New Age shop.

"Hey, Crenshaw, we ought go and check out this dude."

"Whose that?"

"This Ma-ha-ree-she dude."

"What are you talking about, man?"

"Look."

There on the bulletin board of the little shop hung a poster for the Beatles' longhaired, bearded, meditation teacher.

"Hmm . . . the brothers I used to hang with in college talked to me about this dude. Meditation, that's what it's all about. I gotta find out more about this meditation thing."

I saw those signs and recognized my deep interest in meditation right alongside a persistent fear of investigating it. It was a fear that was similar to what I felt going to the Catholic mass in boot camp, the fear that breaking some taboo was going to cost me.

As destiny would have it, the small Omaha base closed, and I was forced to make the "right" decision about where to be stationed. I could go to the East coast or the West coast, to a ship.

My dad's stories were about ports that were accessed from ships on the West Coast, so it was to the West Coast I would go.

I reported to my ship after flying to Andrews Air Force Base in the Philippines. In Subic Bay, my ship's overseas homeport, I boarded the *USS Halsey*, a big, grey, guided missile frigate. There were Terrier missile launchers, deck-launched depth charges, and three-inch fifty canons whose cold steel, small, child-sized shells I'd carry in my arms during replenishment details.

Having arrived in Subic Bay toward the end of a WestPac (Western Pacific) cruise, we visited places such as Kaoshung, Taiwan, and Hong Kong. Hong Kong, a busy cosmopolitan city, was just New York City in Chinese and catered to all the wild things any young sailor would ever want.

A few friends and I walked down the stairs to one swanky night-club in Kowloon and filled our senses with the sights and sounds.

"Hey, Crenshaw, what do you see, man?" asked one of the guys.

"Wow, this place is pretty fancy. Look at the bars spread all over the joint."

"Whooaa!" went several voices in unison.

What was so obvious was easy to overlook.

"Look at those bartenders."

Each one of the small bars encircled a gorgeous, topless Chinese bartender. I'd never seen such beautiful women before up close, and definitely not half nude. Stunned, I wasn't so sure if they were just that lovely or just a lot better looking than the six hundred guys I had been bunking with on the ship. After all the excitement in places like this, it was back to San Diego.

Back in San Diego, I remembered my deepest longing, because suddenly I was beset with something I'd never experienced before, loneliness. There were sailors, men just like me, wandering the streets looking for something and not knowing what.

Were bars and beautiful, inaccessible women what I was really searching for?

I searched the bookstores looking for something to read, know-ing I should stay sharp, keep learning, if I wanted to return to school on discharge.

What do I read that will get me ready for my return to school? Better yet, if only I could find that book that could teach me what I really wanted to know.

And then it happened. I walked into a little bookstore that I hadn't passed before. The lady who managed the store smiled at me and nodded as I entered.

"Good afternoon sailor, what are you looking for?"

I didn't know how she knew I was a sailor, I was dressed in street clothes and looked, I thought like a normal citizen, but then normal citizens in downtown San Diego were mostly sailors.

"Oh, I'm not sure. I'll just browse."

There was something about the little store: it was small but the headings above the shelves gave me enough latitude for browsing that I might spend my entire afternoon in the shop. Above one of the shelves was the heading Buddhism. I wasn't much interested in Buddhism, but in my way around the store, I had to pass through this section. Even so, a faint sense of anticipation preceded my getting to that section.

After arriving at the section, there on the top shelf was a book that literally jumped off the shelf into my hands: *Buddhist Meditation in the Southern School.* As I leafed through the book, I realized that what I held in my hands had within its cover a body of knowledge that I thought did not exist.

Here is what I've been looking for, guidelines for how to practice meditation. No one has to know. It says its Buddhist, but what the heck, I can take what I want from this little book. This is something I can do in secret, no one has to know.

I was sure I was going to catch a lot of flak about the Buddhist religion, but I felt the meditation practice was something altogether different. I couldn't believe what I read. Meditation was not associated with religion. What the Buddha taught was not a religion. What the Buddha taught was a philosophy, and more than that, it was a way of understanding my existential dilemma. I took the information in as if it were lifegiving water.

This little book made a statement, "If you follow the path, you can be free from suffering."

Wouldn't it be wonderful to be free from suffering? Is my separation from the unity suffering? Is this what I am doing on this planet, suffering? Is my experience and grief associated with racism suffering? Is my loneliness suffering? Is my fear suffering?

My little book forced me to consider these questions. My little book explained that suffering existed, and there was a way to be free without waiting for some far-away heaven. This idea wasn't anything like what I had been exposed to in Love Town or at the university. Someone else had to see what I was reading. It all made too much sense and was too simple and practical. I reread the little book several more times, and each time I read it, I was more inspired than before. Dare I share my little book with anyone?

On board ship, I realized that I did have one shipmate who might understand my find. Bryan, a sailor from Jersey, raised in a religious family, whose dad was a preacher, he'd understand. He had trouble with the contradictions in his religious upbringing, and I thought, if anyone could be a sounding board for my discovery, it would be him. He read the book, and his response was immediate and puzzling.

"Hey, Charles, this book is filled with all kinds of revolutionary ideas. No . . . really man . . . this book is deep . . . but . . . no one can do this."

"What do you mean no one can do this? And, how do you mean revolutionary? My little book isn't talking about revolution."

"Revolution man. You know what I am talking about, social justice. Isn't that what we talk about when we think about Dr. King or Malcolm X."

"But is what Dr. King did revolution? Doesn't revolution always entail violence? Couldn't revolution be an internal struggle?"

In these formative days, the dialogue about revolution would sometimes reach a broader audience. O.B. was what we called the Irish signalman from Boston named O'Brien.

"When the revolution comes, you can hide in my basement," were my cryptic remarks to O.B. when the conversation about revolution came up in mixed company, black sailors and white sailors.

O.B.'s response was, "Crenshaw, you can't really think that a revolution is what's going to have to take place to change America?"

"Oh, yeah, there has to be a revolution for change to happen," I said, still not sure what a spiritual, a peaceful revolution looked like.

O.B.'s questioning remarks caused me to pause: my ideas concerned the white sailors. I didn't intended for it to, but it did.

Where was the oneness that I had seen in everything when I was young? Where had that experience gone? Had I really lost sight of my original truth? Is this what everything has come down to?

Life went on aboard ship, and based on my intuition about my little book's content, I began to sit for meditation on the floor in the berthing compartment when no one was around. The living space slept eighteen men, and contained all their government-issued belongings and little else. It was about fifteen feet wide by thirty feet deep. There were bunks supported by steel poles anchored to the bulkheads (Navy-speak for walls).

It was amazing that it never smelled like a locker, but I swore that after sharing this space with so many guys, I would never live in close proximity to so many men again. I would either live alone or get married.

And then there was the final, telling, WestPac cruise. On the final cruise, we entered the port of Keelung in Taiwan.

"Hey, Crenshaw, you ought to hit the weather deck and see the statue of the woman standing on the hill."

"A woman's statue?"

"Yeah, she is so big you can see her from the harbor."

Making my way to the weather deck, I looked over toward the horizon and saw the large statue that my shipmates called a woman. She stood several stories high, wearing robes looking quite like clothes on the picture of the Buddha I had on the cover of my little book. I was certain that it was a depiction of the Buddha, but I was wrong.

Although not as large, the statue reminded me of the ninety-eight-foot-tall statue of Christ the Redeemer that stands arms outstretched overlooking Rio de Janeiro. To me, the "woman," as they called the statue, was awe-inspiring, and she called to me. On my first shore leave, I headed for the hill where the statue stood. I wound my way around the streets of the town, not knowing any Chinese or the exact directions to my destination. There was really no need, I could see the "woman" from almost anywhere along the way.

When I reached the temple grounds, the beauty of the statue struck me. It looked like hand-carved stone. There were was another, smaller statue of the happy Buddha nearby, with lots of what looked like baby Buddhas crawling all over him.

Kuan-yin, the Goddess of Mercy, the panel near the statue read.

I was taken by the concept of the divine feminine, an idea that was foreign to my upbringing. I wandered around the temple grounds, looking at the monks with shaven heads. My little book had spoken of wandering mendicants, itinerant monks who traveled with the weather and as the spirit led them, all the while mastering their meditation practice. Were these shaven headed monks anything like what I read about, or were they just the trappings of yet another organized religion, something I wanted to avoid at all costs?

One contemplation practice in my book came to mind as I strode around the temple compound. I had memorized, with great relish, something called the Metta Sutta, or the verses on loving-kindness.

This is what should be done by the man who is wise, who seeks the good and who knows the meaning of the place of peace: . . .

Let him be strenuous, upright, and truly straight, easily contented and joyous, free of cares.

Let him do nothing that is mean or that the wise would reprove.

May all beings be happy.

May they be joyous and live in safety.

All beings, in high, middle, or low realms of existence. . .

. . .Even as a mother at the risk of her life watches over and protects her only child, so with a boundless mind should one cherish all living beings. . .

. . .he who is made perfect will never again know rebirth.

I didn't quite know what it all meant, but it struck a chord in me. I had never read anything that knew this hidden part of my heart the way these words did. I didn't have to conceal my longing anymore—someone, somewhere knew it.

What I had unknowingly left hearth and home for was found, and the beginning of the end of my long journey was set. I knew what to do with what I had seen. The people at that little temple were real, not just words in a book. How much did I have to learn? Leaving Taiwan this time was a turning point. Our ship made its way to Japan, where I was to begin my transition back into civilian life. The crew had a brief shore leave before it sailed back to its overseas homeport. As my floating home pulled away from the pier, I promised the brothers that I'd "Keep the faith." That pang in my heart was there. The pang of attachment.

My last few days in the military were an unsettling reintroduction "to the world," back into regular United States culture. I learned that upon discharge that I was eligible for unemployment. I also learned about something called affirmative action. In the discharge barracks I had been just one sailor among many. As I lay in my bunk one afternoon, I overheard two men's discussion.

"You know, you are going to go out there looking for a job, and you won't be able to get one."

"What do you mean?"

"The government has passed this law, and any black guy that comes to a job the same time as you do, well that black guy will get the job."

"What the hell do you mean the black guy will get the job?"

"It's called affirmative action, son, and you just better get used to it."

Their discussion turned heated, and I represented the subject of the heat. I left the building discreetly. I walked around the base a few times trying to clear my head and wrap my mind around yet another thing that the culture was setting up to keep the minds of the many in fear.

I'd been trained right alongside sailors from the Philippines, Dominican Republic, and everywhere else. When had anybody asked for a handout? Everybody was the same under the Uniform Code of Military Justice. Everyone took their tests, displayed their skill, and attained rank, if qualified. Why were these guys moaning about some affirmative action? Welcome home, Charles.

By the time I got to my parents' home, I felt disconnected, the only stabilizing theme—school. My younger sister was sixteen, and my brief return to our small half of the double brought with it logistics problems. As much as all were happy to see me, it meant that my sisters would have to share a room for a while. Even though we had always been a tight family unit, my presence was inconvenient. Newly discharged, my new outlook on things creating tension, I called my old shipmate for a reality check.

"Hey Bryan, man, I'm out here and everything is different."

"Like what man, what do you mean different." I told him about the affirmative action episode and other things.

"I no longer 'consciously' accept what the culture says is true. I know it's not. I've seen too much, and add to that my little book."

"Oh yeaaah . . . the ideas from that little book of yours could definitely shake things up."

"You know, I just realized something."

"What's that?"

"I am attracted to Buddhist thought . . . to the ideas in this little book . . . because it doesn't posit a god. It just says work with yourself to overcome your short comings and be happy."

"Hmmm, that's a deep point, man."

"There's no place where this conflicts with anybody's dogma. It's pure philosophy. I don't know why that's important to me, maybe because of fear."

"Fear of what, where do you see fear in your little book?"

"Fear of hell."

"Hey, Charles, I didn't see any hell in your little book."

"I know you didn't, but something inside keeps saying that if I seek the peace offered by meditation, I'm going to hell."

"How can freedom from suffering get you to hell? That's what that little book said when I read it, right?—freedom from suffering?"

"Right . . . right on all counts."

"What's that understanding do for you then?"

"I still don't know just yet. The only real feedback I've gotten from anyone out here is from this beautiful sister at the church down the street."

"Yeah, what did she say?"

"She said, 'I think you're crazy,' which is what I would have said to someone talking like me if I were in her place, I think. No matter, it still hurt."

"Well, what I do know is that the world hasn't changed. You have. You're traveling a road that few take."

Bryan's words, meant to be words of consolation, weren't. What I knew moving forward was that I had to keep my thoughts to myself.

So in the setting of our family's half of the little double, I sat on the floor cross-legged, practicing something that was just not part of the cultural setting: meditation. There was really no place I could sit where it wasn't obvious to anyone passing by or through the room what I was doing.

"What are you doing there?" came my dad's question.

"I'm practicing meditation."

"What's that all about? We don't know anything about this. We don't do this."

I was not able yet to state clearly what I was doing and, most importantly, why. My uneasiness made my dad uneasy. I needed to move on, and quickly, but I couldn't just yet, still not having fully landed in the community or the America that I thought I somehow knew.

I returned to the university less than a month after my discharge. I had that fire that I'd seen in those GIs years before. I now knew what had set the fire that powered their drive to finish their education. I continued my meditation practice, but it was sporadic because of the discomfort I felt at home. Eventually landing a job in the computer operations department for Marion County, a job that one of my GI friends from school set me up with, I was set. With the job and an apartment, I was set to be in close proximity to the deli where I had seen the flyer for the swami.

CHAPTER SEVEN

Doubling Back

Looking to keep myself inspired for meditation, I stumbled across the writings of the Christian monastic Thomas Merton. Merton had written about mystical connections between Buddhism and Christianity, collaborating with D.T. Suzuki, a Zen Buddhist monk. In him, I found an affirming voice, a voice related to Christianity that said my ideas were not completely on the fringe of reality.

I was so enamored with Merton that for a time I considered joining the Trappist order, something that would never be. I spent a few long summer weekends doing silence retreats at Our Lady of Gethsemane in Trappist, Kentucky, totally fascinated by the silent hardworking lives the monks led there.

I awoke in the wee hours of my first full day of retreat and attended the monk's first office. There was some strange excitement at getting up early to go to something special. I sat in the balcony that overlooked the large sanctuary. I was alone. Straight down the center was an aisle that found its way to the huge image of Christ crucified. On either side were, what seemed to be, little stalls where the monks stood or sat as they did their Gregorian chant. On first hearing the Gregorian chant, a flood of emotion swept over me. I sat in the balcony alone, and wept. I had nowhere to place these emotions. They didn't fit with anything I knew.

I returned to Gethsemane as often as I could, sharing the

monks' simple fare, doing silence retreats, and wandering the acreage in search of Merton's hermitage, which I never found. Ultimately I became a familiar of the vocation director, Brother Giles. He was an interesting old soul with deep-set blue eyes that didn't quite seem to be of this world. He was seventy years old when I met him, and had been at the monastery for forty years. He let me follow him into his office one day where I noticed a little book titled *Prayer* by a Swami Abhishiktananda on his cluttered desk. The author's name didn't quite seem to fit with the title, or the milieu. As I puzzled over this, Giles spoke to me.

"Come, let me show you something. I know how interested you are in Thomas Merton. Would you like to take a walk inside the cloister?"

"Sure." I was more than curious to find out more about how these monks lived. As we walked through the rooms' I asked the old monk a few questions.

"Brother Giles, is God in everything?"

"Well, that's known as pantheism. This means that people believe that God is in nature, or can be explained by nature."

"But in a sense that is true, isn't it? God is everything and in everything. Right?"

"No. God is not nature."

I got the feeling from his tone of voice that I shouldn't press him about this. It was more important to me to take the tour than disrupt things based on philosophical differences. We passed through one room where a few monks were sitting, and I stopped the old vocation director with a question.

"What are those stacks of notebooks there in the corner?"

I didn't know why I was concerned about those piles of notebooks, but I was always hungry to read something, expecting to find the missing answer to life's mysteries in a book.

"Oh, those were just things that Father Louis used to teach the novices."

"Father Louis? Who was Father Louis?"

"Father Louis was Thomas Merton's monastic name."

"That's why I have never found a grave marker for Thomas Merton in the churchyard."

"To us, Merton was just Father Louis, and that is how it should have been."

"Sir, what would I have to do to be able to come here?" My curiosity, overwhelming me as we continued our tour, forced this lingering question.

The old monk's eyes widened. "Who's asking this question?" He looked at me to see if I was sincere. My sincerity was misplaced.

"You have to be a Catholic," he said matter of factly. "You have to attend a parish for at least two years and then be recommended by the parish priest if you want to enter the monastery."

I didn't know what I expected him to say, but it wasn't that. Reality hit home.

It seems that only serious Catholics could enjoy the contemplative life in the monastic setting.

"I understand. I can see how the guidelines are established to make sure that no one entered the cloister ill-prepared for the life," I said to the old monk.

You have to become something to become nothing?

I didn't know just how true this was. Our little tour ended, and this was the last time that I bothered the vocation director.

On the way home, I pondered what the vocation director had said to me. What was it I had to become or do? At home, I continued my meditation practice. I also found myself playing bass guitar for a large church choir, in some last-ditch effort to integrate the path I'd discovered with something I was at least a little familiar with. The pastor of the church was a highly educated seminarian who used what I knew to be the occasional Buddhist parable, couched in Christian vernacular, in his sermons. He was a sincere soul who indulged me a few conversations.

"You're a mystic," were the words he directed at me one afternoon.

"I'm not really sure what you mean by that," I said to him.

"You are more concerned with the internal development of your spiritual life."

"Well, I just know that meditation is a major part of my life. If that makes me a mystic, then so be it."

By now I felt, maybe prematurely, that I could teach interested beginners meditation.

"So what do you think? Is it all right to teach meditation to a few interested people here at the church?"

"It has to be Christian meditation."

I was stymied. "What I've learned about meditation, even though I learned it from a Buddhist book, really has no religious connotations ultimately." Wrong words.

The discussion ended abruptly with, "It has to be Christian meditation."

Some days later "Meditation is evil," were the words that flowed from the mouth in the pulpit. I almost jumped to my feet in verbal protest, but contained myself. At the end of the service, I approached and calmly questioned the pastor.

"How can you say that meditation is evil? You have an enormous influence over all these people, both here in this sanctuary and in the broader community by way of radio."

He just looked at me and let me continue my remarks. There were other parishioners standing behind me waiting to thank the pastor for a sermon well delivered and meaningful.

"Why, just down the road a few hundred miles, there are men who spend their lives in meditation, and I've met them. Merton's Gethsemane exists. How can you say these things?"

It took all the courage I could muster to say these things, but they flowed calmly and effortlessly from my mouth. The pastor shook my hand and motioned me along so that he could continue his greetings.

The church was large enough that it required multiple services, and as part of the music ministry, I was around for the second service. The pastor didn't look at me when he came to that place in the sermon, but he didn't repeat those words "Meditation is evil." Ultimately I couldn't reconcile the contradictions between sermons like this and the fire that burned within me.

Frustrated and on my own, I sat on the living room floor of my little apartment and uttered a melancholy prayer.

"Lord, I am at a fork in the road. Is there anyone who can help me, anyone who knows the real significance of meditation? Someone you can send to help me just a little?"

.

CHAPTER EIGHT

The Aryan Controversy

The fire in my gut was for meditation. I tried to reconcile my life as a computer programmer analyst and my life as a contemplative, but something was missing. I changed jobs and started working as a computer programmer analyst for AT&T, Ma Bell. Aside from a lot more money coming in, that was just a change in job scenery. I had to know more about meditation, to experience more, and even with my experience at the monastery, I thought I needed to be somewhere totally dedicated to that. I was half right.

I continued a regimented daily meditation practice at 6:00 a.m., but now yoga postures had completely replaced all the martial arts training after work: sun salutations, triangles, angle poses, warriors, head-to-knee poses with varied leg positions. All of these replaced: counter, strike, kick, punch, snake creeps down, fair lady works the shuttles. I continued rereading my precious little yellow book and others. Many things I read in my books caused turmoil I hadn't counted on.

"You're always sitting there reading. What is it you read so intensely?" said the voice of a lovely black woman whom I'd seen around the lunch room often.

"I'm reading a Buddhist book."

I had seen this lady in the hallways and gone back and forth about whether or not I was attracted to her. Those biological urges. She'd picked up on that.

"What is in this book that is so intriguing? You are reading it like it's the Bible or something," she said.

"It's called the *Dhammapada,* the Path of Perfection, and for me, it is sort of like a Bible."

Our conversations carried on for a few weeks, and eventually she talked me into letting her read my little book. Some books I read contained ideas that weren't much different in their perspective on women than what I learned in Sunday school. Some stated that women were not really qualified to do the practices because they were women. Some even said that women were not able to achieve enlightenment until they were reborn as men. I discounted things like this as another twisted version of the world telling me that my twin sister was some spiritual/religious second-class citizen. My lady friend came back with the *Dhammapada* and pointed out something else, something that was much more difficult to overlook.

"Just what are you reading?" She pointed out the sentence in the book and read, "This work is the product of the Aryans."

I had read that, but somehow it didn't make sense that these ideas had anything to do with the negative connotations that this word held in the world.

"Aryans? Well, brother, isn't this just another brainwashing. This book doesn't consider people of color to be worth anything?"

Fighting past my newly reawakened contempt for the word "Aryan," I continued practicing meditation, because I knew there was something larger than politics and racism associated with it. I was in turmoil for months after this interaction. Was it really possible that I was being duped?

Even with all the mental turmoil, I continued and grew accustomed to doing periods of enforced silence on weekends. I would practice meditation several times a day; read one of the books that I had acquired on meditation, Buddhism, or the life of spiritual teachers such as Yogananda in his *Autobiography of a Yogi;* and be silent. Initially these periods of silence were disconcerting because of an ever-present apprehension. There was no one to confide in.

My meditation practice was simple. My little book said just follow the breath, and when you breathe in mentally, think, "I breathe in peace." When you breathe out, mentally think, "I breathe out peace." It was just that simple. Who knew that the effects of something so simple could be so profound? It was during one of those silent meditation periods that I was confronted with something that would challenge what I was learning.

"Hey, nigger, go home!" a voice bellowed out a second story apartment window as I walked contemplatively along the sidewalk. An unfitting end to a weekend's silence, one particularly filled with peace and serenity.

I recalled my friend's hints of warning. "Crenshaw, where do you live? I wouldn't live there if I were you" came advice that I just didn't pick up on. I had lived aboard ship, and not all the people there were open and friendly. Confronted, as a petty officer in the Navy, with statements like, "I'll not listen to this nigger," there was the Uniform Code of Military Justice to keep most people in check. I was far from the Uniform Code's influence. Being stubborn about being left alone to meditate, I had put myself in an awkward and possibly dangerous environment.

I had read about the things that happened to black GIs on returning home after World War I, and my dad told me about the things that happened after World War II.

"Guys came home from these distant places and saw how differently they were treated. They just couldn't step back into those old shoes. Violence occurred in many places. I once went into a restaurant with some white shipmates. You know what happened?"

"Did people stare at you Dad?"

The waitress said, "We don't serve niggers here."

I was surprised by my dad's story, "What happened?"

"My friends left the restaurant with me. I will never forget those guys for that."

This was part of what was different about those GIs around the card table at the university. Their minds were different. Leaving the States did something for a black man.

I searched the darkened windows over my head to see who had thrown this epithet. There was no face to be seen. What would I have done had I seen the face, seen the exact window? The anger I felt over shadowed the fear; all this outweighed the serenity that was there only moments before. In that moment, I decided that I would stop all this yoga and meditation business because it had no help for me from the hateful mind behind the window.

Struggling with my anger, I found myself at the yoga center searching somehow for answers. Where was that promised relief from suffering that I had read about so much?

"Rose, I have a problem."

"So, what can I help you with?"

"I don't know how you can . . . "

At that point I glanced down at the desk, bewildered about what I'd say. On the desk lay an announcement about a visiting Indian pandit, a Dr. Arya.

"Rose, can I get to see this guy, this Dr. Arya?"

"Sure, he's coming on a Monday night. Is there anything I can help you with 'til then?"

"I don't think you'd quite understand the problem."

I watched Rose write my name down on a list of people who would see this Dr. Arya when he came to town, and a few weeks later the day arrived. When I walked into the little office, there sat a distinguished-looking man with glasses. He was billed as a disciple of my swami, so I thought there might be something useful I could get from him, but I didn't know what. How would he relate to my dilemma, to meditate or to be angry?

I sat down, introduced myself, and in the moment I was moved to ask him a question about his name.

"Pandit, your name is Arya. Does the name have a meaning?

"Why, yes," he said in perfect English, "The word Arya is the root for the word Aryan, and means noble one."

I was relieved by his answer. The truth was that Dr. Arya had brown skin, but he was an Aryan. His words and appearance were a validation that Aryan had a deeper meaning than what the Nazis or the Klan gave to it. After realizing this, I felt right at home telling this man what had happened to me on that contemplative, post-silence walk.

Aside from being misunderstood in my own community, racism was the biggest challenge to my continued practice of meditation. Sadly, I thought, *If this man can't somehow help me, it will be the end to the experiment.*

Dr. Arya listened, more than attentively. His attentiveness was genuine. His expression and his voice were calm.

"You know, Charles, that is your name, right?" as he looked on the sheet where my name was written.

"I have a center in Minneapolis, and I am accustomed to taking walks around the area where the center is located. On more than one occasion, I have been met with the word 'nigger' from someone in a passing car."

I was at once amused and disturbed that Dr. Arya used the 'N' word. I was both ashamed and perturbed that I had to use the word to explain my predicament, but here he was just as conversant with it as I was.

He continued, "It is so unexpected that no matter how much spiritual faith one has, it shakes you up. One time after being confronted in this manner, I returned to the center to guide my regular evening meditation, and I met the center president coming in the door. I said, 'Are you coming to see your favorite nigger?'"

"The president looked at me with shock and said, 'What . . . what did you say Pandit Arya?' I explained the situation to him and then carried on my usual peaceful meditation."

I sat there shocked. Why would someone be so rude to such a lovely man? Dr Arya's timely story kept me from abandoning the practice.

He said, "Only meditation can keep you sane in situations like this."

I didn't quite know what he meant by that, but based on his experience and kind encouragement, I went back to work at my meditation with renewed vigor. In the remaining time I spent in that neighborhood, I was harassed more than any other time in my life, and oddly enough, one of those episodes took on an extraordinary flavor while I was refueling my car.

I filled my car at a gas station a few blocks from the apartment, and one evening at the station I met this old man.

"Fill it up," I said to the old man as he came up to the window I was rolling down.

The old man was a pretty rough-looking old guy, a little more rough around the edges than most people I'd seen at this station. It was a cold evening, so I sat in my car. When I heard the click of the meter indicating I was full, the old man was at my window.

"That'd be eight dolla's, fifty cent."

"Here you go," I said, and I handed the man ten. He all but snatched the money from my hand. It had been a bad stretch of weather, and my windows were filled around the edges with a hardened mixture of mud and salt that made it appear as though I was looking through large portholes. When the man came back, he reached out to hand me my change, and said, "Here's your change—boy!"

This wasn't boy as a term of endearment as my father might use it. It was "boy" used in a demeaning manner and anyone hearing it would know it. I took the change from this old man's hand, envisioning this character dressed in a hooded gown in some lonely field some place. I looked at my change and it was wrong. I didn't want to have any further dealings with this man, but it had to be done.

"You better count the change you gave me," and I handed the change back to the old man. That's when I noticed something strange about him. Suddenly standing before me wasn't an old man, with this hateful persona, but instead it was the swami. The old man, whoever he was, was suddenly mimicking all the mannerisms and the speech pattern I had seen in the swami who had zapped me. I don't know what words came out of the old man's mouth after he handed me back my correct change, I just know that the swami walked away from me and back into the building. I blinked my eyes and shook my head, standing there in the cold. I started up the engine, bewildered, and drove away.

I'm so engrossed in thinking about this swami that I'm seeing him or hoisting my mental image of him onto things that frighten me? Or was it really him testing me about my greatest fear—death by racism?

After a day or so when I thought I had digested the experience, I decided to go back to the station to see if this old man was there. When I got there, I didn't see him around anyplace.

"Hey, where is the old man that works here?" I had no idea what I was going to do if he were there.

"What old man?" the regular attendant said.

"I was here two days ago and some old man filled my tank." I gave him a brief description of the old guy.

"Nobody like that works here."

CHAPTER NINE

Let the Training Begin

More intrigued than ever by what was happening with me, I wanted to learn more about this strange attraction I had to the swami. The meeting with the pandit and a few formal classes in meditation with Rose convinced me that I should take some next step.

"Charles, have you ever thought about initiation?" Rose asked.

She had talked about this thing called initiation in the meditation classes. I remembered the swami mentioning this at our first meeting.

"I have been practicing meditation for so long now, why do I need to do an initiation? Aren't I already initiated?"

Rose didn't have an answer for that, but she continued her thought.

"Well, just for your information, Swami Rama is going to be conducting a seminar and doing initiations at the Institute branch in Glenview, Illinois in a few weeks, and if you want to get initiated, just let me know."

"Oh, the swami is going to be doing a seminar? Now that sounds interesting."

I didn't know about initiation, but I was up for seeing this swami again after my experience at the gas station. What did I have to lose? If nothing else, I could improve my meditation if I spent more time around the swami and really understood what he was teaching. I eventually decided to do this initiation.

"You have to be at Glenview on Saturday morning at 9:00 a.m.

Remember to fast the day before and up to the initiation," were Rose's instructions. "Oh, and remember to take some blankets or a sleeping bag."

A few weeks later, excited, I fasted for more than a day prior to my appointment and then made the four-hour drive to Glenview.

"I am here to attend the seminar and to get initiated," I said excitedly to the cheerful lady who met me at the door, the swami's acting secretary.

"I'm sorry, but Swamiji is not doing any more initiations."

"Wait, who is this Swamiji? I am talking about Swami Rama. Isn't he doing this seminar"

"Swamiji is Swami Rama," she said pleasantly.

"No more initiations? But . . . I came . . . I drove from Indianapolis just for this. How can . . . how could he not be doing anymore initiations?"

"Sorry," she said.

I'd have to see about this. None of this made any sense. Not knowing where to locate Swamiji, as the lady called him, I waited rather impatiently until after the first lecture was over. The weekend was to be filled with lectures and practicum with just swami, and no one else. This event that was to be an extraordinary opportunity now turned sour. After the lecture, the swami came walking back through the classroom alone, and I accosted him.

"Sir, I was told to come here this weekend to be initiated. I did all the preparations and more, and I drove all the way from Indianapolis. Your secretary said that you were not doing anymore initiations . . . "

He stopped me. I was talking rather fast ,hoping to get in all I needed to say before this seemingly busy man had to go on his way.

"Come and see me tomorrow at 9:00 a.m."

It was a simple as that. So the next morning, in great anticipation, I sat outside the room where initiations were being done, and queued up to receive a mantra. As I sat looking through the book I had just purchased, I pondered over the previous day's drama.

Maybe it was all about seeing if I really had the desire to be initiated?

Just then the door opened and the kind face of the swami appeared, and he said, "Come inside, son."

I liked that he called me son. It reminded me of home and my dad. He looked at me with the book in my hand.

"What are you reading?"

I showed him the book. "*A - pa - rok - shanu – bhuti*" I haltingly read. "Self-Realization written by someone named *Shan - kara - char - ya.*"

I would learn later that this man himself had held one of the titles of *Shankaracharya* in India.

"You're not going to find what I'm going to give you in any book."

That's an interesting remark. What does it mean?

The swami went over to a couch in the little room filled with the smell of the swami's favorite incense.

"What is that lovely smell."

"It is the *dhoop* that we burn in the cave monastery I grew up in. The glowing ash we used for light sometime. Come, sit."

I made my way over to the floor in front of him and sat down before him cross-legged, like a yogi. He looked at me with interest; I was very comfortable in the cross-legged position. To that point I had been practicing meditation for six years on my own. He took a piece of paper and wrote something on it.

"Bend your right ear toward me, son."

I did and then he whispered my *guru mantra* into my right ear.

Repeat what I have said," he told me.

I did, several times just to make sure that I had it right. I had never heard Sanskrit spoken, I'd only read it in books. The meaning of that sound had been with me since childhood. Peace, bliss, happiness, divine light, divine love, all sentiments I longed to be sustained in, all part of the meaning of this beautiful sound—the mantra.

"Never tell anyone your *guru mantra.*"

I thought this was a rather curious statement, and failed to understand its import at the time. I looked at the word on the paper carefully.

"Yes sir, I will keep this to myself."

"You should attend our International Congress coming up in a few weeks. You will enjoy the events there."

"I have an obligation that weekend," I said.

I didn't really have a definitive obligation. I didn't want people asking me questions about why I was going to Chicago all the time. Things were weird enough without people actually knowing everything I was doing. I excused myself and told the next person in the queue to go in for their initiation. I left the swami's presence astonished by how the mantra and its meaning had touched something deep inside of me. The morning passed serenely by as I waited for the afternoons events.

In the building, there was a large room where we all practiced our hatha yoga and meditation, where all the lectures were held, and where everyone slept on the floor at night, the men partitioned off from the women. To this point in my experience, I had never met so many people who practiced meditation. All the people that I met were very kind; I was just another aspirant.

In this big room, I saw faces from many different ethnic backgrounds. Several black ladies my mother's age were sitting in the front row of chairs facing the stage. All of these people were long-time students of the swamis, or Swamiji, as I too considered calling him. I found out that one of the black women, Brunette Eason, was trained to give *mantra diksha* (mantra initiation). Trained by one of Swamiji's pandits, Pandit Rajmani Tigunait, she did for people what Swamiji had just done with me. This fascinated me.

Swamiji walked in as I was just introducing myself to these ladies.

"How are you?" Swamiji directed his words to the ladies sitting in front of me.

They all said, "We're fine, Swamiji," in unison.

He began a bit of banter back and forth with these ladies and then motioned for me to come closer.

"Give me your arm."

He reached for my right arm and pulled me closer to him. I was more than a bit hesitant, but very curious about his motives. He held my arm in both his hands.

"Relax," he said.

His right fingers held my wrist and his left ones my elbow. He held the arm as if weighing it. We were positioned fairly close to the ladies in the front row.

What's he doing, what's going on?

He directed my completely relaxed arm over the head of one of the ladies. Once positioned there, he let it go as if to hit the lady in the head with it, and he did. He hit the lady in the head with my arm.

"Hey!" She yelled.

I looked at the swami in horror. I had no idea why he had just hit this lady in the head, a lady I didn't know.

He said, "I didn't hit you. He did," pointing at me.

I was even more horrified.

Oh my goodness, what's happening here?

The swami was gleefully laughing away, and the lady was rubbing her head. After the hilarity had calmed down, Swamiji asked for my arm again.

"Here, give me your arm."

"Oh, no, you don't. I am not falling for that one again."

"Oh, come now, give me your arm." I warily gave him my arm.

"Relax your arm," and he shook my arm a little bit.

Oh, so this must be the test. Now he's going to see if I can recover and be relaxed.

I relaxed my arm completely and he guided my arm over the head of the same lady and once again led it to hit her.

Oh, no, he didn't?

She let out a yelp and said, "Hey, Swamiji."

The swami was gleefully laughing, saying, "He hit you, I didn't."

Little did I know that the joke was on me. That day I learned that the path could be filled with play and joy, it was my choice. At the end of an extraordinary weekend, my car floated south, down Interstate 65 toward Indianapolis without touching the ground, or so it seemed.

CHAPTER TEN

Because I Love You

It was time. I decided to go the place where Swamiji spent most of his time when he was in the United States. His stateside headquarters were located in Honesdale, Pennsylvania. I had garnered a copy of a brochure from the yoga center that read, "Himalayan Institute Quarterly" across the top. I enrolled in a ten-day meditation retreat, and made my way from Indianapolis to Honesdale across the Pennsylvania turnpike. Along the way, I stopped at truck stops to refuel. On the walls of the truckstop bathroom stalls, I saw ample expression of what the men who frequented these places thought of me. As I stood relieving myself, I read one nasty saying after another on the wall.

Why haven't I seen this type of hate-filled writing before? Do I just have a heightened awareness of these things because I am alone, and I feel alone in my search for freedom from this fear?

I continued my way north on U.S. 81 and east on route 6 and into the little borough of Honesdale. I wound my way through the north edge of town and out to the countryside where the Institute was located. As I turned onto the Institute grounds, I was captivated. It was an enchanted valley. The road wound its way around a stack of trees that led to a vista of lush, green, rolling hills. At the bottom of the valley was a huge, yellowish brick building, the type of building that the Catholic church built back in the 1950s. I checked in at reception.

"Are you an initiate?" said the pleasant young woman who was helping me check in.

"Yeah, I am."

"There is the meditation hall up on the third floor above the woman's wing. You have to go down the main hall past the dining room, and, for you, through the men's wing. At the end of the hall, it's three stories up."

I found my way to my room, up the stairs, and down the long dim hallways with their brown vinyl tiles on the floors. Excited about the information the woman had given me, at meditation time, I raced to the meditation hall. Up the three flights and into a room where I found myself among serenely countenanced people, and suddenly they began to chant. Their chant was in Sanskrit, I had never heard such beautiful words in my life.

Siva shakta yukto yadi bhavati shakta prabhavitum . . . came the words from a famous tantric text. I was moved beyond words.

What's happening, I don't know what these words mean, but the vibration in this room . . . This is similar to my experience at Gethsemane, but there is something different . . . How can I get here? I need to be in this place.

These thoughts raced through my mind throughout the ten days I spent there, sitting in lectures with theologians, swamis, doctors, and pandits who had all been trained by Swamiji. On the last day of my retreat, I stood in the hallway with the retreat leaders and Swamiji.

"Sir, how can I help with what you do here?"

The words rushed from my mouth; I had no idea what impelled them. I didn't really want to help, I wanted help. Swamiji was standing across the room, ten feet from me; he walked briskly over to me and put his hand on my shoulder.

"Son, you should consider coming here as a resident for three months."

Three months? How could I get away for three months? I have a job, an apartment. This isn't practical at all.

"All right sir, I'll think about that," I said hesitatingly.

Swamiji walked back to the people he was standing with, and I left the room to begin my return drive to Indianapolis. It would take several years before I was ready to heed his recommendation. One incident in particular helped speed the decision along.

It was a pleasant dream that I awoke from calmly. What did it mean? Swamiji was in it, and there was the familiar entrance hallway of the Institute building. There was something else special about this dream. I had now been to Honesdale several times, and on several occasions, I had heard Swamiji talk about dreams.

"Dreams are the comfort for an unsettled mind."

Aren't dreams part of the normal life of a human being? Don't we all have to dream or go crazy? Isn't this what Freud said?

I knew enough of the common myths about dreams. Every time I heard him make his remarks about dreams, I felt as if he was saying that we were all neurotics. In this case, I was having a dream and he was in it. What could that mean? I couldn't wait to ask him.

In dreams, not everything is clear or remembered, but this dream had an extraordinary quality about it. There were two large wooden doors at the main entrance to the building. Inside these doors was a large room with couches and chairs and the reception area. It was in the space near those large doors that I stood with my teacher. Behind me was the bookstore, with the usual hustle and bustle that occurred during seminars. In the dream, I speak to him.

"Sir, you constantly say that dreams are the comfort for an unsettled mind. What does that really mean?"

He responded with something that I couldn't understand, and then he turned and walked away. As I turned to walk to the bookstore, I looked to my right and saw a woman walking into an office down the hall. This was as much as I could remember. The dream perplexed me like no other in my life.

One bright, sunny morning at the *ashram*, the ancient name for the training place of aspiring yogis, a short time after the dream, I got to ask my question. On that morning, while I was browsing in the *ashram* bookstore, that dream gnawing at me, I vowed that the first chance I got I was going to ask Swamiji about all this. I didn't know whether I should make an appointment to see him with his secretary, Kamal, or just try and catch him. On this fine morning, as I stood there with my thoughts, Swamiji came in through those big, wooden doors at the entrance.

He came in with Justin, one of his longtime disciples and friends, who was physically supporting Swamiji, who had some-how sustained a life-threatening injury to his nervous system. I walked up to where they were.

"Sir, may I ask you a question?"

I always asked his permission to bother him. People were al-ways making demands on his time. I didn't want to be a pest when I could very well do my practice and figure out most things on my own. I knew everything boiled down to direct experience anyway, but I persisted.

"Okay, son, what is it?"

"Sir, you say that dreams are comfort for the unsettled mind. What does it mean when I dream and you are in the dreams? Is this all some goofy wish fulfillment? What does all this mean?"

Swamiji reached out and affectionately stroked the back of my head, much as my father or grandfather would do when I was a child.

Simultaneously, and in response to my question, he simply said, "Son, I am in your dreams because I love you."

With those remarks, and the loving fatherly touch of his hand, my eyesight left. Here for the second time in my experience with my teacher, the entire world slipped away. I was left in some blind-ing, ecstatic, snow-white void where time and space did not exist. It was beyond pleasant. I was in this state for what seemed like an eternity, but which probably lasted only a few seconds, if that long. My usual frame of reference returned only after I notice that his hand is moving away from my head. Swamiji just smiled and con-tinued with Justin down the hallway to his quarters, leaving me standing there in quiet joy and amazement.

Behind the joy and amazement was something else. Shaken, unlike my first extraordinary meeting with my teacher, this inter-action left me physically wobbly. As I made my way toward the bookstore, moving gently as a drunken man measuring his steps,

I realized that this was exactly what had happened in the dream. The parts of the dream that were fuzzy were now intelligible. Moving into the adjacent hallway leading to the bookstore, I saw to my right a woman walking into the accounting office. This was not just any woman. I had a name for this woman; I had met her. I had experienced all of this before it happened in my dream weeks earlier. What was different was the effect on my mind and nervous system. My legs and my arms shook with some unfamiliar energy. I browsed through some familiar books waiting for some kind of integration of my experience.

Swamiji's parting words had been, "I am always communicating with you, you only have to be attentive."

For me, this being attentive was important in dreams. The dreams generally occurred in the wee hours of the morning just before waking. There is something special about the sleep cycle during that time. I got tested in this method of communications many times before Swamiji left his body.

"Swamiji, when you are instructing us in dreams, when you come to us in dreams, will you always come in the form that we know?"

This question was sparked by a dream I had where a person had started out as someone I thought was Swamiji but then morphed into some turban-wearing other. Swamiji turned away from the small group and headed toward the door. I often saw this peculiar response to questions. I always assumed this was done because the person on the receiving end couldn't handle the answer or someone in the room had no need to hear it.

I startled myself by doing something I'd never done. I walked around in front of Swamiji and barred his way to the door. It was not a matter of trying to physically stop him, Swamiji had been trained in kung fu in his youth, and was more than proficient in its practice.

I laid my forehead on his chest and said, "Swamiji, when you come to us in dreams, will you always come in the form we are familiar with?"

He looked me in the eyes and said, "Yes."

I learned that I didn't have to question if he was working with me in dreams or not. My only other preparation for these communications was my consistent practice of meditation. I had no illusions. I knew I wasn't special. Even though Swamiji spoke to each of his students as though we were his most beloved child, he was equally generous to all who accepted his guidance, and not just "his" guidance.

"I am a messenger," he said, I have nothing new to teach. I am only delivering the message of the sages of our tradition. I am a disciple of my master."

Swamiji seemed to be the embodiment of *seva* (self-less service) to the tradition of sages, and generally never acknowledged that he had done or was doing anything special for his students. He always deferred to his master and the tradition of sages.

Once while in his presence, I confessed, "Sir, it seems that my desire for meditation is waning."

He simply said, "I will pray for you," in a deeply sincere voice.

His remarks touched me deeply, and even if the whole tradition was not behind him, here was someone I at least considered a great friend on the path offering a prayer on my behalf. Prayer to God or to the tradition of sages, it didn't matter to me, it was a boon. Swamiji considered yoga a science and he had validated, through his own efforts, many of the things that people read about in books and consider foolishness. He knew a lot about dreams and sleep, and was imminently practical in his application of these things. What he knew was mind-boggling, if to no one else but me.

"The yogis have made many subtle observations about dreams," he began one day. "There are many layers of dreams. There are the dreams where we truly feel that the dream world is the real world, and then there are dreams where you are conscious, know that you are dreaming and can manipulate the dream settings. Haven't you ever experienced this?"

Sure I had, everyone had an experience of this at one time or another.

He continued, "Then there is the level of dream that can be the gateway to the ultimate reality."

I had no idea where he was going with this.

"Have you ever considered how the mind and body are affected by dreams? Take food and sex, for instance, how does your body respond to dreams about these things." He was getting into a sensitive area here—sex. I listened.

"When you dream about food, you are never satiated by the food in the dream, and if you were hungry before you went to sleep, you will be hungry when you wake up. On the other hand, if you dream of sex and are satiated in your dream, then you will wake up satisfied."

Swamiji didn't elaborate on this any more, but it was obvious to me that he was referring to the nocturnal emissions that sometimes happened during sexual dreams. I remembered reading what some monks had written about nocturnal emissions. It was as if they were evil.

Swamiji emphatically stated, "Sex begins in the mind, the urge for food begins in the body." How would I be able to verify that? It made me rethink what I watched in movies and on television. I quietly, but egotistically, questioned all that he said about these things.

Wasn't there something perverse about knowing this much about sex, the body, and the mind?

Then it hit me: I did have some practical experience with what he was saying.

"Charles, do you have a girlfriend?"

"What?" I said, wondering what kind of question this was coming from a chiropractor.

"I said, do you have a girlfriend?"

My chiropractor knew about my interest in yoga, and in conjunction with my postures, he was helping me work through some issues I was having with my body. He had diagnosed a mild scoliosis that had "miraculously" resolved itself with my yoga practice, but what did my spine have to do with sex?

"I ask you this because you come in with the same back issue every time. I see a lot of priests, and they all have the same issue.

As I see it, they have this problem because they don't have sex."

This man could see in my body what was going on in my mind. I had been experimenting with celibacy and fighting with the sexual dreams that arose because of it. If priests could practice celibacy, why couldn't I?

"In all the texts I read, achieving the ultimate goal of yoga or even mystic Christianity, for that matter, requires you be celibate like the priests," I said.

He listened to me, smirked, and said, "Get a girlfriend."

Remembering this interaction with the chiropractor, I realized how little I really knew about my body and mind, and how much I really needed to learn. My religious and cultural conditioning balked at what I heard, was offended, embarrassed Why?

CHAPTER ELEVEN

In the Loving Crucible

My obsession led to the decision to quit the lucrative job I held as a computer programmer analyst. My father thought the decision was more than misguided.

"Charlie, you are quitting a job where you are making more money, at the beginning of your working career, than I made by the end of thirty years working in the factory."

His remarks stopped me dead in my tracks. By then I had a B.S. in computer technology, and I held a management position with the phone company, something I am sure my dad was proud of, though he never mentioned it.

"Yes, sir," I said. "I can't fully explain to you why I have to go, why I have to do this, but I know I have to. Please pray for me."

Dad didn't know about any of the extraordinary events that had transpired up to that point—I confided in no one about these things. No one. Who would understand the kinds of things that were happening, like my dream, my vision?

In my dream-vision, the dreamscape was filled with a golden-orange hue. In the dream, I noticed that my body was going through different yoga postures, some I had no practical knowledge about how to approach. Then the dreamscape went black, and from out of the total darkness, a face emerged, surrounded by this same, golden-orange hue. The man's hair was grey and in what appeared to be small dreadlocks. The face was wisdom laden and golden brown. I searched the faces of men I met for a while after this dream-vision looking for the face I saw in my dreamscape. Some preacher who chided my not finding a passage of scripture in a timely fashion struck me as a possibility for my face, but up close his face lacked the beauty and wisdom I saw in my dreamscape face. Who was that person? I'd never met such a man, but I knew that I wanted to.

Is this what I tell my dad about why I am going? Was this anything rational to tell a man who had made a secure life, seemingly out of nothing, with no high school diploma, a factory worker who expected nothing less than excellence from me in school, and in life?

As fate would have it, at the precise time that I planned to leave, a national strike occurred throughout the Bell system. It was during this time that I slipped away from my life as a programmer. I was going to go to Honesdale as a member of a unique graduate program, something that had been developing in Swamiji's mind over the years. He, like most of the Indians that I met, was a strong advocate of education.

I had been covertly preparing for the change for two years, taking prep classes at the university and seeing where I could sell stuff that I couldn't or didn't want to store. The graduate school was a place to intensify my meditation practice, learn as much as I could about *asana,* and learn the practical science of yoga, yoga therapy, eastern and western psychology, and holistic health—and, get enlightened, all in two years. All but the latter was within reason. Everything boiled down to being practical. Dad would agree and so would Swamiji.

The program in Eastern studies investigated Indian texts related to yoga, vedanta, and tantra, texts with names like the *Yoga Sutras,* the primary text for yoga, *Bhagavad Gita*, the primary text for vedanta, and *Siva Sutras,* a text that related to the philosophy of Sri Vidya. More practical to me, I thought, was the study of comparative psychological methods and counseling, and holistic health with some of the leading minds in these fields. The overall degree was something more practical than just saying I was going to an ashram to sit and meditate. It was a once-in-a-lifetime opportunity.

Unspoken in all this was my quiet fear, my conditioned fear, of traveling alone, of being alone, in my own country (?), where the color of my skin was still a factor. This fear often masqueraded as other things. In my youthful sense of immortality, I had enlisted in the Navy and travelled the world. I was virtually fearless when leaving home, going to boot camp, in those last days of Vietnam. When I packed all my belongings and started the seven-hundred-mile drive to Honesdale, Pennsylvania in August 1983, to be in the company of my spiritual teacher, I wept for the first two hundred miles. I didn't know who or what the tears were associated with; a part of me just observed this intense response to the events as they developed. This was the end, the death of something. I mourned its loss in solitude.

Once I arrived at the ashram, grad school, I unloaded all of my stuff into my room, my cell, as the Christian hermits call them, in the men's wing. Those first few months would be the closest I would ever get to leading the cloistered life that I had read so much about in books. For me, the life was idyllic. Up at 5:00 a.m. to wash and prepare for group prayers and meditation that happened just a few flights up from my room. Those mornings were filled with the beautiful prayers that I memorized, and spiritual readings from individual ashramites. After a while I too participated in those readings.

After prayers, there was asana, asana, and more asana. I reveled in the practice of hatha yoga. Surrounded by people who were more adept than I at hatha yoga, I spent many hours perfecting postures and practices like: *paschimottanasana* – posterior stretch, *shirsanana* – head stand, *mayurasana* – peacock, and *nauli*. Included in those hours was time spent examining the different approaches to practicing asana, and, most important, learning the therapeutic value of the asana, both physical and mental.

Life lessons came along with the academic study of the autonomic nervous system and ancient scriptures. It was, outside my tour of Asia in the service, the most fabulous time in my life and the most terrifying. Passing Swamiji in the hallway one day, I asked him a quick question.

"Sir, I am getting very good at postures, but every time I practice for more than two hours I have this pain here," and I showed Swamiji where I hurt.

"You're overstretching."

"What do you mean overstretching?"

I had grown up playing basketball for hours on end. How could I be over stretching. Swamiji didn't know that I was raised on "Dr. J" and Earl "the Pearl" Monroe, superstars on the basketball court. I had seen these guys do things that I originally thought impossible, but the more I practiced basketball, the closer I got to doing some of the things they did. This yoga business seemed like child's play compared to that.

"The work in asana is different than what you have grown up with," Swamiji said.

"Yeah, well, the best people on the basketball courts were the people who had the tallest, strongest, and most agile bodies."

"Yoga is not about being the tallest or the strongest," he said, "It is about increasing the subtlety of your awareness. Now having said that, you should know that yoga is certainly not for the faint hearted. You should just be aware to stay within your capacity, understand?"

"But Swamiji, I see all these people putting their legs behind their head and doing things that are completely fitness oriented. Are those people increasing the subtlety of their awareness? I am confused."

"You have to realize that the yoga taught by the tradition of sages in the Himalayas is different than the fitness that is being taught. The fitness is really no different than the basketball you mentioned. There is no deeper looking into life, nothing more than having a fit body. Is that really your interest?"

"No sir, I view these postures as means to be stable for sitting in meditation. What I really started all this for is because life as I understood it was a place of great disappointment. No one is happy, at least, I know that I am not."

"Let me ask you something. How old do you think the hatha yoga scene you are learning is?"

"It's thousands of years old."

"Hatha yoga is a more recent development."

I stood there now with my eyes wide and my mouth open.

"Swamiji, you have to be wrong on this," I said forgetting who I was talking to.

"Listen to what I am saying."

I would find out later that any tidbits of information, any conversation you had with Swamiji one on one that lasted for longer than a minute or so, were precious, especially if you were getting your serious questions answered.

"Do you recall the hatha yoga text that you have been introduced to here?"

"Yes, the *Hathayogapradipika*." I was proud of myself for knowing that. "That's the most famous one, but then there is the *Gheranda Samhita* and *Siva Samhita*."

"When was the *Hathayogapradipika* written?"

"I don't know, sir."

"Better yet, how many poses do these texts mention?"

"Not as many as people are doing in the world now."

"Why is that?"

"I don't know."

"It is because hatha yoga as you know it is only a recent development. The poses you know so well are a combination of calesthetics and the original poses mentioned in the text."

"So what does that mean, Swamiji."

"It means that there are two things that are going by the name yoga. One is an exercise regime, pure and simple. The other is a tool for the evolution of consciousness, a tool that provides you with a strong body, but leads you someplace totally different."

Swamiji turned to walk down the hall to his pending appointment, and left me standing there with my thoughts. Information like this gave me pause. When I was done, what was all this going to mean to me, and who was going to understand any of it? Who was going to buy any of this? Even I questioned this man, raised in the Himalayas, whose sole job was passing on, teacher to student, direct transmission, the wisdom of the tradition.

With these life-changing insights, came good food. After morning prayers and postures, there was breakfast, and after breakfast, graduate school classes. After classes came heaven, lunch. I'd never really gotten good, balanced, vegetarian meals before, but I got them at the ashram. We students would sit around the lunch tables and discuss what we were learning with the ashram residents. I gravitated to one classmate, Jim Zielski, a mild-mannered, blond, long-haired vet from Wisconsin who had seen combat in Vietnam. It made an impact on him on a level that I couldn't fathom. I'd seen the same thing in relatives who returned from Vietnam. Our discussions, as we walked up and down the long hill on the campus grounds, ranged from our experience as veterans to upcoming projects in our coursework.

The coursework put us in a unique position for the time. We were to design protocols to verify the efficacy of yoga, something that the National Institute of Health had not yet fully considered in 1983. This was a fantastic challenge, and involved more than just postures, as I would find out.

"You know, Charles, Freud and Jung have never been so intriguing as when looked at through the lens of Buddhist or yoga psychology."

"The Eastern psychology seems to be more intuitive, more like Freud and Jung's take on things. That's why Western scientific psychology has a problem with them."

"So, Charles, what's your research project gonna be?"

"Something to do with breathing, the mind, and high blood pressure, that's practical I think. Jim Bo, I know you love your philosophy even more than I, so I can imagine what your thesis will be." Jim chuckled.

Our training involved lots of things that were totally new to me. I'd read a lot of things about health. I'd done fasts on juice, water, and air. I had even gained some proficiency in doing enemas as an aid to warding off minor illnesses, but I'd never heard of Ayurveda.

"Your constitution is based on three properties, or qualities called doshas."

I'd read about those, they had something to do with primordial elements of ether, air, fire, water and earth, as they envisioned things India.

Dr. Ballentine, a physician and psychiatrist, trained in Ayurveda in India continued, "These doshas—Vata, Pitta, and Kapha—fit quite nicely with body types."

I wondered what he meant by that. On my hearing, it sounded so far fetched. I was to find out that my constitution was a composite of Vata and Pitta, ether/air and fire, a difficult combination. It was knowledge of Ayurveda integrated into our understanding of the postures, physical fitness, and health, as well as a philosophical and psychological understanding of yoga, that made the grad program so unique.

Aside from all the postures, scholarly pursuits and scientific studies was the real everyday ashram life. Living in an ashram was like living in a monastery as far as I could tell from what I'd seen at Gethsemane. I had chores. I washed dishes like a dishwasher at a restaurant in a little room that had great acoustics. I sang as I washed, and all my dishwasher friends enjoyed my tunes. I dust mopped the long, dimly lit halls and swept and mopped the dining hall several days a week.

Living a dream in my ideal setting, still, I had a lot of work to do on myself. The experiences that lay before me were more harrowing than a few wayward dust balls on the long hallway floors.

As a graduate student, I had to get school supplies and other things that were not part of the ashram's supplies. That required going into a nearby town to a big box department store. Common sense, I thought, and fear had made me wary of small towns. Some of this was just the bias that all big city dwellers have about small towns.

As I walked into a big box store on a bright sunlit day in the fall of 1983, I felt lucky that I had the opportunity to be associated with such a unique program, the brainchild of such a unique scientist, physician, and yogi as Swamiji. The decision to go with the program had costs me $6,000 worth of GI benefits.

I recalled the letter I had received from Andy Jacobs Jr., the congressman my mother had put me in touch with. It read:

The Veterans administration respects the fact that it owes you benefits for furthering your education, but does not feel that the program you are pursuing is worthy of supporting. If you choose to change your program to something more conventional like an MBA, the VA would have no problem relinquishing the funds for such a program.

I reflected on this as I made my way to the cashier with my supplies.

"Hi, I'd like to pay for this now," were my words to the cheerful cash register attendant in the department store.

He started to ring up my purchases, and I just looked over the candy to see what I would buy on impulse. In my survey of the candy counter, I happened to catch the eye of a couple a few empty aisles over. This wasn't an unusual occurrence, but there was something about these people. They were looking at someone with such rage and hatred that it was alarming and intriguing to me.

I altered my body position to see if I could sneak a peek at the pariah they were directing their hate-filled stares toward. Positioned as I was, this pariah had to be near where I was standing. As I turned, and glanced, there was no one in the direction they were looking anywhere near where I was. I turned again toward the angry couple and stole a glance in their direction. I discontinued my hunt for candy, and the cashier handed me my purchases.

As I picked up my purchases, I could see that this couple was literally glowing with red-hot fiery rage, a rage that I had never seen before. Directed at me. Remembering my childhood, it was the kind of situation that there was no explanation for, it just was. As I moved, the eyes of this angry couple moved with me. I fled in a panic from the department store with lynch scenes passing before my mind's eye. My greatest nightmare had come to life.

Was I being followed? I had to get back to the ashram now. NO, I had to leave this place now. Graduate school, or no graduate school, ashram or no ashram, I had to leave this area because my life is in danger. It was written all over the faces of that couple in that store. This wasn't like the N word from a second story window. Where was my safety in numbers, who was going to help or protect me? Who for one hundred miles would even understand what I just experienced?

Despite having grown up in America in the sixties, this was the first time I had come into direct contact with people who obviously hated me with a boiling, seething hatred simply because of the color of my skin. I had only seen such hatred like this on the faces of people on TV. Even the foolish, red-headed boy in high school didn't look like this.

I made my way back to the ashram on country roads watching in my rear view mirror for any telltale signs of being followed by these people. I didn't know what I would do if they had followed me.

"Don't be afraid." I remembered Swamiji's words.

But I knew that.

"Don't be afraid—fear breeds danger," came all of his words.

Fear breeds danger? Had I dragged those angry people to the department store and set up this situation for myself?

The lesson was far from over. One night coming back from the small town on the dark country road that leads to the ashram, a car pulled up behind me, right on my bumper. It was a sequence of events reminiscent of something that happened with my family when I was younger:

"Dad, I'm going about sixty miles an hour."

We were on our way back to the motel from a family reunion in Kentucky, late one summer night.

"I'm doing sixty and this guy is on my bumper."

"What?" Dad said as he looked in the rear view mirror on his side.

In my innocence, I said, "I must be going too slow for these country boys on this one lane highway, so I'll just pull over and let this maniac go by."

I started to slow down to pull over, and the car behind me slowed down also.

Dad said, "No, don't pull over."

"I'm just going to ease over to let this silly person go by that's all."

"Don't pull over, Charlie," he said, "There's nothing on the highway that is stopping this person from going around us. You keep going."

I had no idea what my dad meant, but at that point a carload of locals sped around our car and off into the darkness. Dad's family was from those hills in Kentucky, and he knew something I didn't.

Now there I was alone on a country road and there was a car, just like then, tailgating me at high speed. I slowed down and pulled over to let the car go by. Unlike back then, I was driving a four-cylinder car, doing my bit to help the environment, and I wasn't going to outrun whoever was behind me. The car pulled up behind me. There were no blinking lights of the police or any sign of movement from the other car. I fully expected to have to defend my life. No one got out of the car. I sat for a few moments and then started down the country road again with the car still following me but at a safe distance. I arrived at the ashram safely, and the other car disappeared onto some side road. The next morning an ashramite quizzed me.

"Anything weird happen to you lately?" he asked.

"Yeah, man, Some whack job tailgated me last night."

He was holding back his laughter, "Aw, man, that was me."

"That was you?"

For him this was an innocent prank, but for me it was a nightmare. He didn't know about the department store incident. He had no knowledge of my life experience. No one really knew about my life. None of this was in the realm of their experience. I was doing all the prescribed practices, but still I suffered with my fears, and I asked Swamiji about it.

He said, "You suffer because you identify with the things of the world."

These were Swamiji's words and they made no sense.

Do you know what it is like to be black in America?

"You suffer under the delusion that you are the body. You are intoxicated, like everyone else, by the 'I am the body' idea."

What? How in your right mind can you say that I am the one at fault here, what about the racism and bigotry in America? Even India suffered with a similar plague with the British. I'm afraid, I'm suffering, because I did this?

"Out of ignorance you set up this 'I' against everything else. You love what gives this 'I' joy, and you hate what gives it pain. In the end, these two extremes lead you to a fear of death."

Yeah, right, fear of death. That's what I'm talking about. I'm afraid of being killed—death by racism.

"What dies? What is afraid of dying?" Swamiji continued.

"I die." *What kind of silly questions were these?*

"The body dies," he said, "Have you ever seen a dead body cry out in pain or tremble with fear?"

"Well, no."

"So then, what is afraid of dying?"

"The mind?"

"Precisely!"

"But how does that explain my suffering, my pain?"

"You identify with being black instead of identifying with your true self, your true nature, and you suffer."

I knew that there was a profound truth in what he was saying. Profound ideas were all through the books like the Yoga Sutras and other philosophical and psychological texts that were required reading for us. I just didn't know how practical this kind of thinking was for my life situation.

My lessons continued and got harder. Still, the ashram was a relatively safe but challenging environment to work out all sorts of things. As the days rolled by, the issue of the thesis for matriculation loomed before me. In classes such as research and statistics and self-regulation, topics for my study would pop into my mind.

"So, Charles," said one of my advisors one morning, "What will be the subject of your thesis?"

"I want to investigate the effects of yoga and meditation on high blood pressure."

"That's an interesting condition that breathing and relaxation has had a lot of success with."

"Well, my dad suffers from hypertension as do many other people in my family and the community I grew up in. I thought it might be worthy of some research. Maybe I would find ways to help with this health problem."

"The bio-psychosocial perspective on health and illness is what you are talking about here," my professor continued.

"And just what do you mean by bio-psychosocial, professor?"

"Here is an example. When rats were put into an environment, and the population got too large for the area, they developed all sorts of conditions. One of those conditions was high blood pressure."

"So even if high blood pressure developed, how is that related to anything?"

"Well, the research suggests that because of the stress of over-crowding, things like high blood pressure and other psychosomatic disorders developed."

I knew that word—psychosomatic. It meant that the disorder was created by your physical and mental habits.

"Eighty to eighty-five percent of all illness is psychosomatic," the professor went on.

Swamiji was the expert here. As a scientist himself, he had offered himself up for study by other scientists in the late '60s, when the wave of swamis and lamas from India and Tibet came to America. He was among those with names like Maharishi, Satchidananda, and Trungpa. Swamiji had done things such as stopping his heart, and he just generally confounded scientists with his complete control of his involuntary nervous system. It was Swamiji, trained as a physician and master of himself, who was confirming these statements about psychosomatic illness, so I paid attention.

The things I learned in my investigation into the psychosomatic origins of high blood pressure proved to be disturbing.

"One of the ways that blood pressure is raised is repressed anger," my instruction continued.

"Professor, can you give me an example?"

"An example? Well, say a person has something done to them, and it makes them violently angry, and they don't express it and just sit on it. That could be an example."

Oh my god. Was it possible that the high blood pressure in my community was due to repressed anger or anything like that?

"A great majority of the population has high blood pressure, and we are learning more and more about its psychosomatic origins, and the issue is more than just proper diet."

Ahhh! The thought flashed. *I can't continue this line of study. This is terrifying. The implications are too great. If I were even slightly on track with my understanding, who would believe it? Who would accept it? Could it really be true that the hypertension in my ethnic group, an ethnic group that by far has the highest incidence of high blood pressure, was based upon its collective response to social pressures, explained here so nicely under the heading of a bio-psychosocial phenomena?*

The thought of it was too much to bear. Research for the high blood pressure study opened my mind to truths that just wouldn't go away. The floodgates of my unconscious opened up, and all sorts of thoughts and questions plagued me, and surfaced in the most serene place at the ashram, the meditation hall.

Hey, what are you doing here? Look around, there is no one here who has to go back out into the world and face what you have to face. You're wasting your time here searching for some fabled release from suffering, some fictional enlightenment. Inner peace? What inner peace? You better get your behind out of here!

Stokley Carmichael, Malcom X, Nelson Mandela, and Dr. King were all present in pieces inside me, but the implications of Dr. King's dream held the highest position, and it was from this I took inspiration to piece together a philosophy that kept me moving forward.

Yoga is about transcendence and self-mastery. What did this have to do with everything else I had learned? What did yoga have to do with being black? What did the sense of unity have to do with yoga? The sense of unity that I experienced in the backyard at seven, it made sense then, but why doesn't it make sense now?

"You suffer because you identify with the things of the world, and per the sages, the mind and the body are things of the world," Swamiji's words came forward.

Here, at the ashram, confronted with all my doubts and fears, I wanted to escape. I had simply wanted to be at the ashram and work on my enlightenment. Often, in terror, if obvious to no one else but myself, I pressed on.

I read about some of the practices that Swamiji had been required to do in his youth. Sitting at charnel grounds was one of them. The charnel grounds were places of cremation, or where bodies were left to the animals and elements.

"Swamiji, what would you do at the charnel grounds?"

"Master would assign me different practices."

"And how does this type of work help you with the fear of death?"

He didn't have to answer that question. I had read that the Buddhist monks did practices on the stages of decomposition of the human body. Somehow I knew that this would be a good deconditioning practice, a good prelude to learning to leave the body consciously. One of my secret aspirations, after first hearing about it, was to leave the body consciously, and I knew that understanding death was key.

Swamiji went on, "The charnel ground experience was necessary for certain personality types. There were those who needed to get beyond their sensual nature, or their pride, or just simply their attachment to their body."

I would get challenged about my attachment to body and ideas constantly while living at the ashram. One such challenge occurred during a weekend seminar between me and a psychiatrist, a professor at Wayne State University.

"How do you categorize yourself?" he asked. The professor was visiting for a seminar with my professors, and his specialty was high blood pressure and its causes in the black community.

"What do you mean, how do I categorize myself?"

"I mean, you are here at this place, and there are no black folk here, that I can see, but you. This philosophy you are learning, you talk about the ideas and philosophy so comfortably. How do you categorize yourself?"

I paused, but I was clear in my response, and what I said came from my heart and not my head, I thought.

"I consider myself first a spiritual being, next a human being, next a man, and lastly a black man."

I didn't quite know the real implications of what I said yet, but it was shades of the child in the backyard.

With great consternation, the psychiatrist looked at me and said, "That's a problem. You are in America, and the way you view yourself is going to get you hurt."

I thought back to my frightening experience in the department store during my early days of grad school, considered what the doctor said, and considered what I had learned from Swamiji. The masters would send their students to the charnel grounds to work out their fears, of death and other things. Charnel grounds full of decaying corpses, and burned bodies. I had found myself in the charnel grounds examining my fears more than once. Leaving home and mourning for the first two hundred miles, arriving at the big box store charnel ground, alone, to deal with my fear of death and attachment to body and ideas. I was forced to confront the skeletons of immoral ideology, and the decaying corpses of hatred and intolerance, and much more.

More than once I started to leave, but I never did, and only the gods know why. There was something more, much more important than running away.

*Above: Charles with Swami Rama
at the Himalayan Institute,
Honesdale Pennsylvania.*

Below: A Himalayan yogi's cave.

Left: Charles with his wife Carol

Below: The Stupa at Sarnath, the site of the Buddha's first sermon.

Vandana Mataji and the entrance to her ashram

*Right: Charles demonstrates
nauli, one of the six cleansing
practices common to both
hatha yoga and Ayurveda.*
Photo by H. David Coulter

*Below: Charles demonstrates
the peacock pose.*

CHAPTER TWELVE

Just Foolishness?

Ashram life was intense for everyone, and for me, an occasional respite from studies and inner work was a trip to New York City. Only a two-hour car ride from the ashram, there was always a student or two who wanted, or needed, to take an excursion into the big city to visit the center there, and maybe pick up a yoga class from some of New York City's notable hatha yogis.

On one excursion into the city, as I walked along 14th Street at 6th Avenue, my eyes paused in a doorway that led up a flight of stairs. What caught my attention was the man in the video preparing to do a headstand, something I had become quite proficient in, I thought. He set himself up using his hands, but then he lifted his hands and stood on his head in a completely unsupported headstand, in the middle of the floor, no wall, no nothing.

I spoke to the man standing at a stall in front and to the side of the doorway selling costume jewelry, who saw me with my mouth agape, "Hey, do you see what this guy is doing? What is this place?"

"Oh, yeah," said the man, "This is Yogi Dharma's studio. Go up and see."

This was my introduction to Yogi Dharma, the man made famous by his extraordinary prowess at hatha yoga and his world-famous poster. Outside of my ashram education in asana, this was one of the first "true" hatha yoga masters I had met. The other one Swamiji himself had introduced us to, Swami Bua.

The fascinating thing about Swami Bua was that he was ancient.

"Well, I am in my eighties and I practice asana about eight hours a day," he told an audience of astounded onlookers at a conference. Swami Bua went on to explain his life story.

"When I was young, I was very sick, my body was badly deformed. At one point, I was taken to the charnel grounds as dead and prepared for cremation. A yogi, who noticed that I was not dead, just near death, came to my rescue. He nursed me back to health with hatha yoga, and through this training brought my twisted body to the normal appearance you see here today."

These were the types of people I was exposed to, and they reminded me of the things I had learned in graduate school, reading the Yoga Sutras, and what I'd heard Swamiji say.

"On the path of raja yoga, asana is the third step after the preliminaries. The essence of yoga, as well as all the religions, is to be free from your fears and abide in your true nature."

"So, Swamiji, what is my true nature, my true self?"

"Happiness."

It was as simple as that, but I was still far from understanding it experientially. Part of the meaning of my guru mantra was happiness. I wondered how all this fit. I still had to take care of some basic, albeit ill-considered, basic human needs, which for me meant getting married. I discussed the marriage idea with my mother because I had an unusual dilemma.

"Momma, there are some very nice women here," is how the phone conversation began on the subject of getting married.

I had become friends with lots of people, and living in an ashram setting, everyone gets to see you in all types of settings from work to play. The diversity at the ashram was not as great as when I had been in the service, but it was there. My service experience had me consider what it would be like to marry an Asian woman, but my question for my mom was somehow different. She heard the questioning tone in my voice.

"The only problem is that none of these nice women are black."

Momma didn't pause a second before she said, "Well, honey, you have to do what is best for yourself."

I was surprised at her remarks, but they came as a relief. I didn't have to feel guilty about considering a woman who wasn't black, at least in front of the one black woman, aside from my sisters, that meant the most to me. The illusion of race was a huge source of conflict in my ethnic community, and much more than just some curious sociological phenomenon you'd read about in sociology textbooks. I found out how real and confusing this dilemma was in my own family history while sitting around the dining room table one day with the women in my family.

"Whose picture is this?" I asked my mother and sisters as we looked through some old family photos.

"Here's Aunt Hortence, Aunt Nan, but who is this other white lady?"

"It's Aunt Buddy," Neenee said.

My sisters looked at me as though I was from the moon.

My younger sister, Fancy, asked me, "Where have you been?"

"Okay, ladies, you always know the inside story on these things. I always seem to be the one left out. What's the real story about this woman?" The woman looked so familiar, but she was obviously white. I imagined that being the wanderer in the family, I had missed out on some family discussion where things like this were brought up.

My momma sat next to me and spoke to me in that tone that she used when she was going to divulge a story like the John Taylor story, so I situated myself to hear something extraordinary.

Momma said, "That is a picture of your Aunt Buddy."

I had heard about Momma's sister who died, and I had seen a picture of her when I was very young, but the picture looked nothing like the one I held in my hand.

Momma went on, "She looks like a white woman because her father was white."

The picture I had seen when I was young definitely indicated that Buddy was mulatto, and a very fair mulatto at that, but so was my grandmother. All my grandmother's sisters looked like her, and were pretty—yella—women, as they were called in the neighborhood, having varying blends of African and European features.

"Your grandmother fell in love with a man who got her pregnant. She wanted to marry him, but he wouldn't marry her because she had black blood. Buddy was the product of that love."

This family situation flashed before me some time later when Swamiji returned from India and questioned me, "Charles, where is your girlfriend?"

"Swamiji, I don't have a girlfriend." He was on me about the conflict in my mind. All the books I read had influenced me on some level, and I still struggled with the idea of being celibate versus getting married, right along with the issues of ethnic identity. What a heaping mess.

"You should get to know Carol better."

It's not that the idea of such a relationship hadn't crossed my mind. Carol and I had been friends for some time and had even discussed the fact that she thought she should marry a nice Jewish man, and I had similar thoughts about marrying a nice black woman. Neither option was available to us at the time.

"Swamiji, I have known Carol for a year and a half or two years now."

"Good," he said, "You can get married right away."

What would I say to black folk who asked me why the woman I married wasn't black?

With this thought came terror. Terror of getting married, or social ostracism, or the fear of death, I couldn't tell.

I posed veiled questions about my conflict to my yoga philosophy and yoga psychology professors.

"How would you explain an inferiority and a superiority complex?"

"They both revolve around the illusion called the ego."

"Is it the ego that fears death?"

"Right. The ego, the mind, creates the fictions called inferiority or superiority."

"So if someone is afraid to die, it is not their true nature that is afraid of this, it is just their mind. How do you overcome this?

"Meditation, and grace," came the cryptic answer.

I was working hard on my meditation. I got that—what I needed was some grace.

"So if there are these thoughts in your head during meditation that are screaming at you that you are wasting your time, or that you are misleading yourself, that is the mind?"

"Your mind, your thoughts, and your ego are the same thing."

Still, I struggled with my attachment and all the confusion it entailed. It was as much a struggle with death as anything else that I had gone through up to that point.

Swamiji was relentless in his efforts to get me to make a decision about marriage. In public lectures, he would call me out.

"Sir, about the nature of the mind in Yoga . . . " he'd stop me mid-question.

"Son, have you decided yet? Where is your girlfriend?" He didn't answer any of my questions on any topic. He just kept pressing his questions, those things that plagued my less-than-conscious mind.

By this time, I had become friends with Jerome, the only other black person who spent more than a weekend or two at the ashram during my initial years there. He was the only person I could identify in any way with what I was going through. Once, while we were walking and talking together, we bumped into Swamiji, who joined us as we walked. I could never have, in my wildest dreams, conceived of what was about to transpire.

Swamiji began talking in a voice completely free of its usual thick Hindi accent, in a style more akin to the way Jerome and I were talking.

"Jerome, can you believe this? There are women here who like him, but he won't have anything to do with them because they're white."

My heart stopped. Here was this man whom I had the deepest respect for, respect truly on a par with my own father, a man who had looked into my heart and saw my deepest, anger-hidden fear and conflict and was calling me on it.

"I never said that," were my first quick words.

I had barely even dared to say it to Jerome. It was an unspoken truth between us. Even after having the conversation with my mother and knowing what I knew about my own family origins, this idea, this fear still held a formidable power. I stood in my teacher's presence, ashamed of my feelings. Why was I lying to my teacher? It wasn't really a lie, there was more to it.

Fear drove my mind to the worst, the murder of a fourteen-year-old boy named Emmet Till by two white Southerners, a boy who was not much older than me in the '60s. The two men, who were acquitted, later boasted of their killing in a national magazine. The boy had whistled at a white woman.

"Well, yes, sir." Ashamed, I amended my remarks and admitted my fears. "That's true, but these people are crazy."

I stood there with my entire heart laid open, my deepest terror exposed. *Had any soul ever stood before their guru harboring such feelings and made it to enlightenment?*

Swamiji simply said, "What people, who's crazy?" He knew well what I was concealing from him. I trusted that he did and that he wouldn't make me explain this all.

"Yes," he said, "This may be true, but Carol is not crazy." He continued, "Once I arranged a marriage between two young professionals. The family's were from different castes, and one family's color was much darker than the other. These young people struggled with issues similar to yours."

As he talked, my mind raced. *Even you can't fathom this one, Swamiji, this is not about your caste system. How can you know my plight here in America? How can you know the demons that I have had to struggle with to even be here? Even your profound knowledge can't help me with this.*

My heart sank as I considered these thoughts. I'd been raised in a state that, in my youth, had harbored America's largest population of the terrorist organization the Klan. It was always an issue for me, just as Malcom X had insinuated. No matter how far I excelled in my education, or social or professional status, I was still this pariah. The anger and the fear associated with these feelings lay hidden.

It's interaction's like this, with the teacher, that move students to run away, saying the guru-disciple relationship is lunatic. This is too much.

I stood there understanding that my teacher was trying to help me, and not knowing how I was going to overcome the hurdle.

We continued walking. Swamiji didn't stop with his assessment of my conditioning, he continued by working on the level of the male ego. After he had stopped me in my tracks with his first remarks, he said, "Are you a sissy?"

He didn't ask me if I was afraid, his were words straight from the streets where I grew up, fighting words. This beautiful old man left no portion of my fear, anger, or confusion concealed. On several occasions after this walk, Swamiji would chide me.

After a few of these rather startling interventions with Swamiji, he mentioned to the doctors that I had a complex.

I had a complex? Why would he say that to these doctors?

This was the psychological reasoning behind my responses. I knew this all too well from my training. Understanding the mind from an Eastern and Western psychological perspective made me more than aware that what he said was right.

One final episode on this issue was to be the crowning jewel, and it occurred when Swamiji, walking down the hall toward his quarters, called out to me, "Hey, Charlie, come here."

He was one of the few people who could get away with calling me Charlie. In his voice, there was always somehow the familiarity of my dad calling my name. I walked toward the door in the hall where Swamiji stood. As I neared him, he wrapped his arm around my shoulders, and we continued to walk down the hall through the glass-paned door.

No one understood what I was going through trying to make this decision about marriage. One of the professors, well intended, although having no clue of my life experience, said to me, "You're just being selfish."

I wanted so much to explain to Swamiji why I couldn't or wouldn't consider marrying Carol. Everyone assumed that it was just because of the usual male looking for a superstar model or something. Carol was a lovely, thoughtful woman who had a particular trait that I admired. She was someone who beat me to the meditation hall. I still wanted to make sure that my teacher knew everything.

I started to explain my fear, "Swamiji do you . . . " I was cut off mid-sentence.

"Son, you suffer because you identify with the things of the world." I'd heard this before.

"You told the visiting black professor that you identified as a spiritual being first, but your main identity, unconsciously, is as a black man."

No it isn't . . .

I had been practicing meditation for ten years at this point, and I still didn't fully accept all the facets of my mind.

Exasperated in anger, the words came tumbling out, "If I cease to protect this body, it will be killed. How do I cease this identity?"

"Continue your practice of meditation. It is this unconscious identity, this conditioned identity, that prevents you from considering the qualities of Carol as a mate, and prevents you from regaining that awareness of oneness that you remember. Ultimately that oneness is the only thing I am here to help you regain."

And then, a final, fascinating conundrum.

"Son, you will look all over the world for the rest of your life, and you will never find a woman who matches you as closely as this woman matches you."

How can you say that? I looked and listened in utter astonishment. He followed his statement with what may have amounted to be the most startling words he would ever say to me, "Don't run away."

Out of fear, mental conflict, confusion, I tried to. Someone was needed to help in the bookstore in New York City, East West Books. Having received my graduate degree, I volunteered for what I thought would be a slight pause from the pressure, but I wouldn't escape my training.

CHAPTER THIRTEEN

East is East and West is West

With my meditation practice and my work at East West Books in New York City, I slowly started to sort things out. It took one year for me to integrate what my teacher was trying to help me understand about myself, and about getting married. New York City was just what the doctor ordered, with its variety of ethnic groups and assortment of worldviews. Women from all over the world passed through our store in that one year, from TV stars to ordinary mortals. It dawned on me one day that aside for what we had in common with meditation and yoga, it would take years for someone to get to know me as Carol did, and years I didn't have to waste.

During that one-year interim, I tried to explain my inner turmoil to my friend and future wife, but I wasn't very successful, and I didn't know how to be.

"You know, it's difficult for any human-being to truly understand another. I know that you can't truly understand the kind of turmoil I am going through."

Carol listened quietly on the phone.

"You know, my twin sister doesn't fully understand me, nor do I fully understand her. And I have known her my entire life."

I drew on the longest-standing relationship with a woman I had in the world for some means to explain my position, and continued.

"How could I expect for you to understand what I am struggling with."

Where was I going with all this? When Swamiji returned in the spring of 1986, things miraculously came together. Carol and I were finally married in a Vedic ceremony performed by Pandit Rajmani Tigunait, surrounded by family and friends, on August 17, 1986. We then found ourselves in the New York City outpost of the Himalayan Institute, challenged in our work, but content together.

In that one-year interim before getting married, I had begun my training on the proving grounds of New York City. I spent months alone in a small room above the bookstore and yoga center, and adjacent to the Center for Holistic Medicine. I ultimately wore many hats while serving the guru at our New York center, mostly all at the same time. I saw patients as a yoga therapist, and taught yoga and meditation classes to Wall Street analysts, schoolteachers, Muslims, Christians, Jews and atheists. Eventually I would see clients as a hypnotist.

Not too many steps from where I was helping people was also where I lived for a while. Like many old buildings in Manhattan, the one at 78 5th Avenue had its problems with roaches and mice. One morning while meditating, something tickled my leg.

Okay, your mind is playing its usual games and you just need to focus. You just need to sit here with your head, neck, and trunk erect and let the mantra do its work.

This tickling sensation began moving. *Maybe it's a roach? Whatever . . . they don't bite. Stay focused.*

Unable to resist, I very slowly opened my eyes and turned my glance down toward my right leg folded under my left. I couldn't see anything. I slowly dropped my head a little to get a better view of my entire thigh. Looking down, I saw a full-grown mouse sniffing at my leg.

The space the Institute was renting was zoned commercial, there was really no space set aside exclusively for living. My room was makeshift at best, and aside from my clothes and the small bed that was brought in, I was sure that this room was the mouse's regular field of operation, and I was the interloper.

As for my work in the bookstore, I was often in the position where both praise and curses would come in the same day, and sometimes in the same hour. Working with the public in Manhattan was a tough practice.

"Excuse me," said one stately, graying gentleman one morning. I'd never seen him in the bookstore before. "Just who is the book buyer here?"

This was an odd question, and one that sometimes preceded strange remarks. I had gotten used to them. Not everyone thought that the comparative study of religion, philosophy, mysticism, and alternative medicine was a valuable field of study. I was the buyer, and the doctors and scholars who had trained me thought that the store ought to represent the cream of the crop from these disciplines.

"Can I ask you, sir, what's your interest in speaking to the buyer?" The man may have been an author or sales representative for a publisher.

"Well, I just wanted to commend that person. I work at the Vatican and I go to stores like this all over the world. The selection of books in this store is one of the finest that I have seen in the world."

I was both surprised and a bit embarrassed. I knew I wasn't solely responsible for the selection of books, but I did have a hand in selecting some of the eight thousand titles that we had. I was also very proud of what the man said about our store, our outpost for distributing ideas. Our store was a haven for seekers of all kinds from Richard Gere, Wesley Snipes, Rae Don Chong, Tom Hulce (Academy Award nominee for Amadeus,) James Coburn, and many other notables, including Goldie Hawn.

My meditation practice and study fostered ideas about divinity and oneness, ideas I had held since childhood, protected from the arguments of skeptics. Those ideas were able to begin to flower again in the milieu of ashram life and also within the confines of an extraordinary, nontraditional seminary that trained rabbis and "interfaith" ministers. It was here that my feelings about unity in diversity saw the light of day again in my mentors and colleagues. It was a welcome supplement to my training in grad school and with my teacher, and a boon to my experience with meditation.

The New Seminary was the brainchild of an extraordinary old Hasidic rabbi, Joseph Gelberman. Among its illustrious cofounders were Swami Satchidananda, founder of Integral Yoga, and the Reverend John Mundy a student of Helen Schucman, the channel for *A Course in Miracles*. It was there that I got my formal, practical introduction to the world's great religious traditions.

"Tell us your name and the tradition you represent," said the rabbi on the first day of classes.

"My tradition is Jewish, or my tradition is Islam or Wiccan, or Bahai, or Indigenous," came the words of my classmates.

One nurse told her story.

"I would go to mass every morning," she said. "I would be so moved by the sense of holiness I experienced that I was happy to go about my day of service in the hospital."

As she continued her story, I was saddened. She had such a sweet experience with her "Christianity." My experience with the whole of the Christian tradition had not been so heartwarming. I was saddened and intrigued by the contrast in our stories.

"Charles, what's your tradition?" the rabbi asked, as it came to my turn. He would ask me this question many times over the five years that I studied directly with him.

"Rabbi, I don't play the religion thing. I'm just Charles." He would just smile.

After one of my usual responses on this subject, the rabbi asked, "What do you mean by that?"

"I don't really have a desire to be a minister. I'm fascinated that the seminary teaches that all religions have a core value that is the same."

"Yes, they all have an unfathomable experiential aspect, something the mystics ultimately have no words for."

The rabbi knew about mystics, being Hasid, a mystically oriented segment of Judaism. Sadly, he was an outcast in his community of origin because of his stance on the things we were talking about.

"The mystics, like yogis, they don't fight over the names that they use to express themselves."

"No, they don't. It is the outer trappings of religion that people make war over. Things like rituals, myths, and social conventions." The rabbi paused. "Speaking again of religion, where do you fit in Charles, what is your mother's religion?"

I paused, undone, with no smart answer in response to his question posed in this way.

Rabbi went on, "Charles, your religion is that of your mother; how she prayed, and where she worshipped floats in your veins. So tradition has it that even though you may not acknowledge a religion, you are born into one."

"Yes, sir, I understand," I said to the rabbi. "My mother is Christian."

"What you have concealed in your heart does have a place in the world," said the rabbi cryptically, "And maybe you'll find a way of expressing it."

The teachers taught and I absorbed. The sufi read from the Koran, *La illah ha illallah,* and translated, "There is no reality but the reality." The priest, Father Giles, read from his Jerusalem Bible, "The kingdom of heaven is within." My rebbe, as I started to refer to the rabbi, spoke to us about the divine feminine, the *Shekinah,* and the teachings of Kaballah.

The Methodist minister, Jon Mondy, spoke to us from *A Course in Miracles,* "Nothing real can be threatened, nothing unreal exists, in this lies the peace of God. Swami Satchidananda, citing the Vedas, reminded us that, "The truth is one but the paths are many." The *Voodou* high priestess spoke of her tradition, something I would inevitably need to know more about. The Wiccans spoke of their traditions and the Native Americans theirs. As varied as they were, no tradition went without respect.

The seminary's goal, not widely accepted, fostered the transcendent unity of religious traditions, clearly a major part of the rabbi's worldview. This approach to world peace often met opposition.

The seminary house was located in the West village not far from the Christopher Street subway station. You could easily miss it as you walked by on any given Saturday morning because it was located in what was the garden apartment at 54 Barrow Street.

When not functioning as a seminary, the precincts of the seminary house were home to the Little Synagogue. Having been raised Hasid, the rabbi was never far from some interaction with the Torah, or the Baal Shem Tov, or Martin Buber.

As you walked down the ten or twelve steps to the seminary, watching your head as you entered, you couldn't miss the *mezuzah* at the threshold, or, after entering, miss the Torah's storage area behind the podium. These things marked the place as a true synagogue.

"Would you please be quiet, sir?" said one of my classmates one day to the little man sitting at the back of the room by the door. He was short with dark, curly hair and beady eyes. He wore a brimmed, black beanie cap, and was dressed in dark clothes. His countenance wasn't very pleasant, but he wasn't an ugly man.

"You're telling me to shut up?

"Sir, I only asked that you . . . "

"Woman, you shouldn't even be in this synagogue. You have no right being here learning from a rabbi."

This then set off a wave of abuse directed at the rabbi, who was at the podium, and at my classmate sitting a row up from the doorway. I had seen the administration dealing with this little man before. There always seemed to be a disturbance when this little man was around, and I never knew why. The rabbi had seen this man before, but what troubled me more was how this man treated my classmate.

If this woman were my sister, which, in essence she was, would I stand for him saying such things to her? Wasn't he being disrespectful in the synagogue and to the rabbi?

I got up from my chair and approached the little man.

"Stay back, what do you want?" said the strange little man as I approached him. I continued toward him, and he stood up from the chair where he was abusing my classmate.

"I'm warning you," he said, "I know karate."

"Yeah, right, right. You are being disrespectful to my classmates and to my teacher. If you don't like what's going on here, you shouldn't come. Will you please leave?"

"You son of a bitch!" He raised his voice, as if to give himself power. I had heard worse on the basketball courts and in the service, and I'd been called worse in the bookstore.

"Go on, go on, leave, we're not bothering you here. How are we harming you here?"

At this, the only other male student in the room at the time came to my assistance. I wasn't planning to physically throw the man out of the building, but I firmly intended to coax him out of the space.

"You two . . . why . . . you faggots." He spouted more of his venom, but, glancing over his shoulder at us, worked his way up the stairs and away from the seminary house. I never got a clear answer from the rabbi why this man had it in for him.

The rabbi simply said, "There are many ways people strive to quell the light of peace. This little man is a henchman for disharmony."

With the man gone, the rabbi continued his teaching, seemingly unaffected.

I found no greater pleasure than gathering at the seminary with those I considered wise, no matter what their religious background. Swami Satchidananda, the rabbi, and Swamiji were all more than familiar with each other.

I was once assigned to accompany Swamiji on a guest speaker appearance at the seminary and on leaving the speaking venue with Swamiji, he confided in me, "You know son, the rabbi is a very loving man."

That evening I got a chance to see the mutual admiration two of my heroes had for each other. I also got the chance that evening to be completely alone with my guru.

Why should such a physically powerful man need an escort, even though I'm honored? Could it have been just a matter of protocol, with me being on the lecture faculty at the seminary, or was it something else?

As we rode along Sixth Avenue headed back uptown to the hotel where Swamiji was spending the evening, he spoke with the taxi driver.

"Hello, son, how are you?" The driver, noticing Swamiji's thick Hindi accent, his appearance, and being from India himself, he responded to Swamiji's question with a quick, "Tik," Hindi for okay.

Swamiji said, "I know you." He looked at me and said, "I know him."

The driver looked into his rear view mirror to see if the face in the back seat was a familiar one. I sat in utter amazement watching the face of the driver as Swamiji told him how he knew him, most of the conversation readily easing into Hindi. It was as if they were old friends from India. The driver had no idea who Swamiji was, but he was totally captivated. I was still puzzled by all this "I know you" stuff.

As we walked back to Swamiji's room, I asked him hesitatingly, "Swamiji, what just transpired in the taxi?" not really knowing how to ask him such a question.

Swamiji, almost interrupting my thinking, said, "I knew this man from another life." I wasn't really on board with that explanation. I'd been around Swamiji at other times when he'd mentioned reincarnation.

"It's not really reincarnation," he said. "What you people call reincarnation is really rebirth or transmigration. Reincarnation implies a conscious moving from birth to birth. Usually people die and are reborn unconsciously into new circumstances."

Swamiji would often say things that were hard to figure out, and seeming impractical. At the ashram during many of his tennis exercise sessions, facilitated by my guru brothers and sisters with whom he played, little pearls of wisdom, pearls for our bewilderment, would be dropped like bombshells.

I spent a total of nine years working in the trenches of New York City, eight with my wife. I was yoga instructor, janitor, counselor, therapist, bookstore manager, and more. I saw some of the dark underbelly of the city as well as some of its brightest lights. People stole our books and sold them on the street corners in front of us as their first amendment right. Our store was burglarized three times. We labored on. We felt we were in New York as a rehabilitation center for those seeking a balanced life. The proceeds of our work went to supporting the ashram and its global charity outreach.

I loved the books and the opportunities to study in New York. The New School for Social Research was just across the street, literally. I continued my counseling studies there, studying alcohol and substance abuse. Sadly, the frenetic pace of the city wore me down. Every chance I got, I would ask Swamiji when we could be relieved of duty. The answer from Swamiji was always encouraging but never what I wanted to hear.

"Be patient, I have a few projects for you here."

It was during this time that I got a chance to interact with the spiritual teacher Ram Dass, author of the classic *Remember, Be Here Be Now,* and other books. There was one book in particular that caught my attention from his early writings, *The Only Dance There Is.* It was here that he made a few remarks about black folk and yoga. At first reading, never having met Ram Dass, his words seemed those of an out-of-touch, privileged, American male intellectual, born in the 1930s. He wrote that there was some interest in yoga among black folk on the coasts, West Coast more than East, and little to no interest in the middle of the country.

It wasn't until a brief but defining private conversation with him, during a book signing at the store, that I decided that he wasn't really this out-of-touch elitist. Ram Dass stood with me in a small office, with his broad, mustachioed smile, bright eyes, and balding head; he was a much larger man that I expected him to be based on the photos I'd seen in books. As we waited to go to the large room where he was to sign books, I spoke with him about his guru.

"I know of your guru, Neem Karoli Baba."

Ram Dass's eyes sparkled, and his face lit up when I mentioned Neem Karoli Baba.

"How do you know him?"

"Swami Rama writes about him in his autobiography. They both spent a lot of time around Rishikesh. I have read many of your stories about your interactions with your Baba. They seemed so familiar."

As we chatted, I recognized that he had an understanding of the profound effect a real guru can have on a seeker. Such were the days at East West Books.

In 1993, Swamiji finally responded differently to our request to leave New York.

"You know, son, you should come to the hospital and do some service there."

I wanted to go to India, but I wanted more to get out of New York City.

"Yes, you should come to India, but not just yet. You have debts to pay."

"What debts do we have sir? Our car is paid for. We rent an apartment, and getting out of the lease would be no problem . . . "

Swamiji had gone on from there in his mind. There was no answer to my questions. I would soon find out what debts he meant, though.

Carol's father, Pop Goldie I called him, became terminally ill about halfway through the next year. The night before Pop Goldie left his body, he and I watched his favorite basketball team, the New York Knicks, lose the NBA championship while I held his hand.

He said to me, "Charles, I don't know what else to do." He had already been through one surgery that left him on life support for a few days, something that he despised.

I said to him, "It's okay, Pop, it's all right, you don't have to know what else to do. There's nothing else to figure out." These were my last words to this lovely, old Jewish man who treated me like his son.

Carol was with her father the next morning when her stepmom arrived at the hospital (her biological mom had died when Carol was thirty years old). Upon her stepmother's arrival in the room that morning, Pop Goldie saw fit to leave. After these events, everything opened up for our departure to India.

CHAPTER FOURTEEN

A Prelude to Practice

Arriving in India with my wife and only a sketchy idea of how long we were supposed to stay, we made our way, with our tour group, to Rishikesh, a six-hour bus ride north of New Delhi. The tour had great plans to visit Gomukh and Gangotri, famous pilgrimage sites, and places of *sadhana* (spiritual practice) for Swamiji, but these plans didn't pan out. Political unrest in the country prevented it. Everyone stayed in the Hotel Ganga Kanare, on the banks of the holy Ganges, everyone except Carol and I.

Kamal Didi, Swamiji's trusty secretary came with a message.

"Yo, Charles-Carol." Kamal always jokingly greeted us this way, as if our names were one, "Swamiji wants you to report to Sadhana Mandir Trust."

"Kamal, what is that, where is it?"

"It's the ashram that Swamiji founded, and it is just a kilometer down the road. He said you should come now."

"But we have to get our room situation straightened out first."

"No, that's just it, that's why I'm here. You're going to be staying at the ashram, not here in the hotel."

We were driven down the road to the ashram that the locals called Swami Ram ashram. The ashram manager greeted us just inside the gate.

"Hello, my name is Prem," came the bubbly voice of a graying, slightly bald Indian man who obviously, from his speech pattern, had spent a good portion of his life in England.

"I'll show you to your quarters." He led us to one of the rooms designated for couples, not far from the main gate. The ashram was beautiful. There were flowers—roses, marigolds, dahlias every-where—guava trees, and lush grass. It was an oasis of tranquility not quite twenty-five yards from the Ganges. Shown our room assignment, we started unpacking.

"Carol, this room is a bit dark don't you think?"

"Yeah, but we'll get used to it."

"Hmmm, it's September," I said, as I swatted a mosquito away.

"September, so what about September?" Carol asked as she started to open her luggage getting situated for our stay.

"It's September and the mosquitoes are still in full force. We don't have any mosquito netting with us. We going to have to sleep with one eye open to fight 'em off."

Carol laughed. Mosquitoes didn't bother her like they both-ered me.

The next morning, still drowsy from my night's combat with the mosquitoes, I experienced my first bucket bath. Along the road from Delhi to Rishikesh, I'd seen more than one person tak-ing a bath by a free-standing water spout or in a stream. There was something earthy and natural about it that I liked, so I had no problem with the idea of filling my bucket the first morning at the ashram. I fancied myself in a Himalayan cave performing my daily ablutions, preparing for the day's round of begging for food and then *sadhana*.

"Oh, no, there's no hot water," I said.

"What do you mean, no hot water? How are we supposed to bathe?"

"I don't know, but I'll speak with Prem. I wonder what the yo-gis did about hot water in the caves?" I chuckled. I hunted the ash-ram manager down and asked him about the hot water situation.

"Prem, our hot water heater's not working." He looked at me quizzically.

"What do you mean, hot water heater?" I thought this was a pretty straightforward statement, but I had forgotten, Dorothy and Toto weren't in Kansas anymore. We were in the land of Oz.

"We were trying to run water to bathe, and there was no hot water."

"Oh, you mean the geezer?"

"Geezer?"

Prem laughed, "Okay, let's go over and see what you have. Do you know how to cut it on?"

"Cut it on? You have to cut this geezer thing on to get hot water?" I didn't want to be the annoying American, but this geezer business was news to me, and I had been around.

After some tinkering, Prem discovered that the geezer was out, and it would take a few days to get it repaired. He later moved us across the yard to another room that just happened to be much brighter, drier, and with fewer mosquitoes.

After that cold, first-morning bucket bath, we found out that everyone at the ashram assembled underneath the tent that was in the courtyard. The courtyard was the only place where stones covered the ground. The tent provided a soothing respite from the sun's midday intensity. The schedule was that Swamiji would come and visit with the ashram guests every morning before going to the hospital.

We went out and took seats under the tent, and shortly thereafter Swamiji appeared and took his seat in front of the eight of us who were staying at the ashram at the time.

"So, son, I see you have finally come," Swamiji said to me.

I bowed toward him with palms together.

Hey, I was the one who kept asking to come and you were the one who said wait, wait, so I don't quite get it. I smiled, puzzled by his remarks.

"You and Carol are here because the ashram is where the meditators stay." I didn't quite get that meaning either, but I was in a way honored that he said it.

"How long will you stay?"

"Swamiji, we didn't know what to do about visas, so we only got six-month tourist visas. So that means that we have to be gone from here by February."

"*Yes*, I see," he said. "Here is what we'll do. You and Carol will stay until I tell you that it's time to go. Okay? You go now to the Ganga Kinare and meet up with your group, and every night you come back here."

"Yes, sir," we said with palms together, and we made our way to the hotel, on foot.

Things went this way for a couple of weeks. The political unrest left our group stranded at the hotel, with Carol and me tucked away at Sadhana Mandir. Although it wasn't scheduled, Swamiji came every night to lecture at the hotel, to pacify the group's discontent. He apologized for the inconvenience we were experiencing.

The hotel's basement conference room and the hallway leading to it, trimmed with dark brown wood fixtures, had dim but adequate lighting. The conference room itself had a makeshift stage. There were chairs for those who needed them, and cushions on the carpeted floor for others, the norm for such a crowd.

One evening as Swamiji sat on the stage, a stage with no special lighting, something curious happened. A golden white light began to radiate from inside the body of our old teacher. Mystified, I looked away, certain that the visual anomaly would go away after a few refreshing blinks and refocusing. I looked again at Swamiji seated on stage barely twenty feet away from me. He was still glowing. I remembered my experience shortly after initiation.

During initiation, Swamiji suggested that I might like to attend the International Congress held in Chicago. This was a large event the Himalayan Institute hosted every year that brought together experts in yoga, spirituality, spiritual traditions, and what would come to be known as integrative medicine. I decided at the last moment to attend.

I met Swamiji in the hallway one morning as he was standing in the doorway leading into the large auditorium. Surprised to see me, he put his palms together and nodded a hello. I haltingly put my hands together to respectfully return his gesture and paused there, amazed and confused at what I was witnessing. There he stood in his Nehru suit, his grey hair neatly combed back, gesturing and glowing, glowing this most beautiful golden white light, from the inside of his body outward.

There he was sitting on stage in the basement conference room of the Hotel Ganga Kinare glowing the same way. I had no reference for my first experience, but I did for this one. What I also had was the benefit of someone else who might be seeing what I saw.

"Carol," I whispered to my wife as I leaned over toward her, "Do you notice anything on the stage?"

Certain that she was going to say no, I prepared to just chalk the phenomenon up to something I couldn't explain to anyone.

"Yeah, I see a light or something coming from Swamiji."

I looked at Carol and remembered what Swamiji said to me years before: "You will look all over the world and never find another woman who matches you as closely as this woman."

So we are both lunatics. I laughed under my breath.

As people began to disperse after the lecture, I discreetly asked around, a few people here and there, people I felt comfortable asking my strange question, "Did you notice anything during Swamiji's lecture?" Two people said that they had observed some light coming from Swamiji at one point.

The days rolled by, and through a series of misadventures, by tour's end, my wife and I had contracted amoebic dysentery. After one completely missing day, a day vacillating between running to the bathroom with diarrhea and lying in bed in a near-unconscious stupor, my wife had an idea.

"I have Dr. Barb on the phone. She wants to know your symptoms."

"Did you tell her I was sick?"

"Well, yeah. You are pretty sick, and those pills for diarrhea that Prem gave you obviously aren't helping." Carol's symptoms were some eighteen hours behind mine. She wants to know if you want to come to the hospital?"

"I really didn't want to go to the hospital, I was hoping the symptoms would pass." These symptoms I wouldn't wish on an enemy, if I'd had one, things flying out of both ends with bloody diarrhea down below, and fever. In a fog, I said, "Yeah, well maybe it would be good to go and get a little medicine for this diarrhea."

Prem ordered us up a cab.

When the cab came, I stumbled out of bed in a daze, hardly knowing where my clothes had been stored. The bright, midday sun blinded me as I emerged from our bungalow. I crawled into the back seat of the Ambassador, and sprawled out next to Carol. I don't know how we got to the hospital. It was a twenty-five-plus kilometer ride from Sadhana Mandir to the Himalayan Institute Hospital.

The hospital campus was vast. There were to be beds for hundreds and hundreds of people and state of the art technology. All of this was to help the underserved village people in the surrounding Himalayan foothills. It was destined to become a hospital with a medical school.

Dr. Barb, the hospital's head of homeopathy, met us at patient intake and was our mother hen, from testing to room assignment. As we sat in the waiting room awaiting our test results, sitting still was not something that I could do.

"Barb, where is the bathroom?" She directed me to the open door I could see down the hall. I came back with greater urgency in my voice.

"Dr. Barb, where is there a bathroom I can use?"

"What do you mean? I sent you to the bathroom. What's wrong with the bathroom? Is it not clean?" Dr. Barb started to look around for someone to send to the bathroom to check its condition, and she started to direct me to another bathroom.

"I can't use the bathroom that you sent me to. It doesn't have a toilet in it."

Dr. Barb looked astonished and chuckled at my Western expectations. So far, I had been in environments that catered to the Westerner. Now I was in an environment with the real people of India.

"Charles, the most natural way of relieving your bowels is in a squatting position. Get back over there to the bathroom."

I had completely forgotten about the toilet arrangements I had experienced while in Asia during my stint in service some twenty years earlier.

With the results being that we both had amoebic dysentery, Carol and I were assigned to a room in the private wing of the hospital as Swamiji's guest. The hospital was not yet completed, and our room, with its whitewashed (light, whitish-blue painted) walls, had four beds, and we took two side by side. The days of our convalescing began.

"Carol, if I could sketch, I'd show you the most marvelous things," I said to my wife as we lay in our beds one night.

"You're really sick, just rest."

" Rest, I can't rest, I keep running to the bathroom."

Between bathroom runs, I was occasionally seeing figures in the wrinkles of the sheets. One night I was able to explain to my wife just exactly what I was seeing.

"I see these three faces. One is facing me, the other two are facing, one to the left and the other to the right. The one on the right is fierce looking, the one in the middle looks benevolent, and the one on the left looks sort of neutral."

She listened, as a wife would to her delirious husband, and did not respond. She was hardly well enough herself to clearly assess my seeming loss of sanity. One morning I woke up to another enigmatic sight.

As I lay, facing the window, the early morning sun coming in, I looked to the whitewashed wall nearest me and saw two figures quite clearly. The first was something half-monkey and half-human. This confused me. I had no point of reference for this. The other figure was unmistakable. It was Shiva sitting cross-legged, his right hand holding rudraksha beads, cobras wrapped around his neck as garlands, with his trident nearby. Everything about him was clearly defined, not like the other form I saw.

"Carol, remember I was telling you about the things I was seeing?"

"Yeah, why? Have you seen something else?"

"I just saw this half-man and half-monkey on the wall, and I saw Shiva in full regalia."

"Oh, the half-man, half-monkey could have been Hanuman," she said.

I wrote these things off as feverish, dysentery-evoked delusions until asking Swamiji about them later. When we were well enough to begin some light exercise, we bumped into him on the road.

"Swamiji, I saw Shiva on the wall of my room, and a half-monkey, half-human something."

"You saw Hanuman on the wall. You know . . . Hanuman, he is the chief devotee and servant of Sri Rama the hero of the Ramayana."

"Yeah, that's who Carol said it was. I would never have related what I saw to Hanuman, but I had no doubts about Shiva. Swamiji, why is it that I'm not seeing Jesus, Mary, or Joseph instead of these deities? Since I was raised Christian, why shouldn't I see images related to the tradition I was born into?"

"I can't answer that for you, you will have to understand this for yourself. What you have seen is very auspicious."

What I neglected to ask him about were the three faces in the sheets. I'd only realize later that they were Brahma, Vishnu, and Shiva after seeing a stone carving, almost exactly like the faces I saw in the wrinkled sheets. There were a few other things I hesitated to ask Swamiji about during our stay at the hospital, and these were dreams, dreams that, in hindsight, I was ashamed to ask him about.

The dreams occurred after an unusual occurrence as I lay in my hospital bed one night. The bloody diarrhea had stopped, and as I lay in my bed, there was a tingling up and down my spine, a soothing tingling, like bugs crawling up the spine. I greeted this simply as the body being urged to heal itself with the homeopathic remedies Dr. Barb was giving us. Later that night came the first dream, and I tried to explain it to Carol the following morning.

"Carol, I've had sexual dreams before, and I thought I knew what they meant, but the dream I had last night stymies me."

"What happened in the dream?" Carol was good at helping me think through the symbols and images in my dreams.

"This dream was a nightmare . . . I think . . . I don't know." There was this large, coal-black woman with long hair down her back sitting astride a man, and they were having intercourse.

"So why was this a nightmare? Who did the people represent to you?"

"It was a nightmare because that woman wasn't normal. There was something special about that woman. Maybe it wasn't a nightmare, maybe . . . maybe it had some important meaning."

"What kind of meaning?"

"I don't know. Now that I'm talking to you, I think the coal-black woman was the goddess Kali. Swamiji was in the scene."

"What was he doing?"

"He was down in the corner of the dream as an inset pointing and what seems like urging me to understand what the scene meant."

The next night I dreamed again.

"Carol, I had another dream. This one was just as freaky as the one last night. In the center of the scene was a fiery, white-hot, molten pillar of light with faces on either side of it, one male and one female."

This image was clearer to me than the image of Kali, and less terrifying.

"The man and the woman were both licking that white hot pillar with their tongues, the woman on the left and the man on the right. They were both of African descent." I continued, "And just like before, Swamiji was there in a little inset in the scene."

"What was he doing this time?"

"He was pointing at the scene, at the couple's actions, just like before and urging me, with facial and head gestures, to understand what was going on."

CHAPTER FIFTEEN

Sadhana at the Mandir

A few short weeks later it was back to Sadhana Mandir to finish what we started, a six-month meditation practice directly monitored by Swamiji, a once-in-a-lifetime opportunity. Carol and I settled into a quiet little routine.

Our bungalow had a twelve-by-fifteen foot main room where everything from sleep to asana and meditation occurred. On the south wall by the windows was my bed, and Carol's was on the north wall, with a four-foot-wide, eight-foot-tall multi-shelved storage unit between the beds on the east wall. The white tiles on the bathroom walls, up to my shoulders and on the floor, gave what was an otherwise drab-looking bathroom a bit of character.

It's 3:30 a.m., and my wife and I are awake in the cold, dark room. Watchdogs are barking outside, as if they are a recording being played nonstop over loudspeakers. Sweat pants and sweatshirt by the bed, I hurriedly put them on and make my way to the bathroom in the dark.

What's going on here? I remember this.

I find the light in the bathroom and immediately turn back to the main room to light the candle for meditation. Returning to the bathroom, I wash my face,and brush my teeth with an animated fascination, and expectation.

Washing done, we both settle in on our cushions, wrapped in hats and shawls against the cold, to begin our meditation. I remembered:

I crept quietly across the little bedroom in the darkness, inching my way over to the other bed in the room where my twin sister, my closest friend in the world, lay sleeping. I was five years old, and there was this fascination about doing something in the pre-dawn darkness.

"Neenee, get up, wake up. Let's get ready . . . "

Neenee woke up rubbing her eyes and stretching, wondering what I was up to whispering in the dark. We shared the room in our modest little house.

Waking up, Neenee blinked at me wide eyed as I stood there in the dark in my pj's.

"What'd ya want? Why you wakin' me up?" she said as she stretched. She'd been coaxed into more than one of my little escapades. There was some mystery in why I needed her to help me complete the task.

"Come on, Neenee, let's get up and wash and get ready," I said, whispering.

"Get ready for what?" my sister complained in an audible voice. I had no answer for that, but does any five-year-old boy on an adventure?

"Shhh, Shhh, we don't wanna wake up Momma and Daddy." There was some internal delight, something fascinating about that early morning darkness. My sister rolled out of bed and stretched again, her eyes now finally acclimated to the darkness.

"Okay, we hav'ta be quiet goin' by Momma and Daddy's bed, so tiptoe," I whispered.

As we eased into the middle room that separated our room from our parents', every step was a question. Creeeaaak, went one of the floor boards as we made our way.

"Shhh, Shhh." I put fingers to my lips that my sister couldn't see in the darkness.

She whispered, "I didn't do that."

"Shhh, Shhh."

Our parents' bed was right at the edge of the doorway, and Momma's all-pervading presence was on the side closest to the door. How would we ever make it past her? Slowly we crept, barely breathing, past our parents, asleep in their big double bed, and quietly down each step, undeterred by the darkness. Our house was barely five years old, not as old as we were, and we weren't sure, just yet, which steps would creak when stepped on.

At the bottom of the stairs, the bathroom was just a few steps away from the landing. When we finally got to the bathroom, we cut on the lights and began running water to wash our little faces.

Something special's supposed to happen when we're done. We're supposed to do something.

"We better run the water slowly so we don't make any noise," I said to Neenee, who was being a good sport about all this. The bathroom in our little house was located right across the hall from the open stairwell right below our parents' bedroom. We didn't think to close the bathroom door. An alert parent could easily hear any noise. All washed up, we stood with bright shiny faces, ready to get dressed for the day.

"What next?"

"Hey Neenee, let's go back up stairs, and wait."

"Okay," she said.

The hands on the lighted clock read 4:30 as we crept back past our parents' bedroom. We were up even earlier than daddy would get up to go to work. We made our way back to our room, put on the clothes laid out for us for the coming day, and sat in the dark on our beds.

"I'm getting sleepy."

"Me too, Neenee, let's lay down and wait."

Nothing happened, and in the interim between darkness and dawn we pulled the nice warm spreads up around our ears. When Momma pulled back the spreads to get us up, those once-shiny faces were crumpled with sleep again.

"What on earth have you children done?" asked Momma, looking at her nicely ironed clothes now completely wrinkled.

"We got up early momma, to get ready!"

This is what was supposed to happen that morning with my sister! I remember what to do in the early morning darkness.

After the morning meditation, an hour or two of asana practice, then breakfast. After breakfast, we climbed twenty or thirty steps up to the top of the walkway, an embankment that separated the ashram grounds from the river, and we set out for a long walk alongside the Ganges. There were all sorts of things to be seen in and around the Ganges, from wild elephants across the river to tightly wrapped corpses floating down the river toward the dam. These corpses, retrieved before entering the locks in the dam, were deposited at a nearby charnel ground where they were handled quite neatly by the vultures that hung around the area.

After our walk, there was japa, which sometimes meant nap, and then lunch. After lunch, a short walk, more japa and study, dinner at around 7:00 p.m., a couple of hands of two-handed solitaire, meditation practice, to bed, only to start it all over again the next day.

As the seasons rolled on from fall to winter to cold, we had to modify our sleeping arrangements. We went from sleeping under blankets to sleeping in sleeping bags. The bungalows were nestled close to the Ganges, making them quite damp, and when the mist rolled off the Ganges at about 2:00 a.m., it was bone-chilling cold.

As part of our practice, we were both taught *yoga nidra*, and *agni sara*. *Yoga nidra* (yogic sleep), is a practice, when perfected, allowed you to experience deep, dreamless sleep while being totally aware and alert. The rest received there occurs without passing through the dream state, at least this is how we were trained to approach it, not that we had perfected it. Swamiji had demonstrated complete mastery of this state and had demonstrated it for scientists. I approached Swamiji with some questions one morning under the tent when only Carol and I were at the ashram for a few days.

"Swamiji, when I do *yoga nidra* I get very deeply relaxed but that's all. What am I missing?"

"Tell me what you do, are you deviating from what I taught you?"

I explained to Swamiji what I was doing.

"I exhale from crown to soles and inhale back to crown, from crown to ankles," and so on, indicating to him all the major points of inhalation and exhalation. "But nothing happens that I can tell different from meditation."

"The secret to *yoga nidra* is sushumna," he said. It is also an overlooked aspect of meditation, and the reason people have such a hard time progressing."

"So that's the missing link. You have to have mastery of sushumna to really do the *yoga nidra* you are accomplished at. This is about more than deep relaxation."

With this ,Swamiji got up to go about his duties at the hospital.

Agni sara (the essence of fire), on the other hand, was a very vigorous and demanding abdominal exercise. It created intense heat in the lower abdomen and pelvic area, and had some other unusual side effects.

The order for this exercise was simple but challenging: apply the root lock, exhale, start contracting the lower abdomen, controlling the contraction up to the navel, smooth and steady. Then all the air out, deep chin lock, abdominal lift and hold, all to release in reverse order. I knew the routine well. Swamiji had recommended that one hundred repetitions was a good number to shoot for.

The practice produced intense heat in the body and built strength in the lower abdomen and muscles of the pelvic bowl, something that could come in handy for a martial artist or tantric yogi. I recalled pictures of Shaolin monks dragging heavy stones with their reproductive organs. Ouch, but this was all part of knowing the body on all levels.

The order of things in the daily routine was *agni sara* first then *yoga nidra,* and that was the sequence one morning about a month into our stay. During the final stages of *yoga nidra,* an intense warmth lit up my spine. Reminiscent of the tingling spine while convalescing at the hospital, this was a much more intense, but soothing, fire from the base of the spine, up to and flooding the entire brain. At that moment I was neither awake nor dreaming.

Swamiji was inside the door of our bungalow in his usual red *yakota,* standing at the foot of my bed asking me a question.

"Son, how long will you stay?"

The same question he'd asked the first morning. His time frame for when we should leave had been more than vague.

"Sir, our visa says that we can only stay for six months."

"No, you will leave after more than one year."

"All right sir," I said in the dream.

When the dream (?) was over, I told Carol, as she finished her practice, what had happened.

"So, what do you think it means," she asked me.

"Well, he did say not to leave until he told us to on the first day, remember? This seems like a pretty convoluted way to tell us exactly when to leave, though."

We both wondered out loud about the dream for a few days, and then we forgot about it.

As the days rolled by with nothing to do but practice and study, I embarked upon extended periods of *trataka* (concentrated gazing at a candle flame), and I increased my understanding of *swara yoga,* the science of the *swara,* the breath and the *prana.*

The *Shiva Swarodaya* read, "The breath from the nostrils reflects the subtle element that is dominant in the body," and "The *swara* is connected to the cycles of the moon." All that I read seemed like allegory, just like some of the stories in the Bible. I experimented with what I read, thinking initially that I'd only find mischief in the pages of the text.

Day after day, along with all my other daily activities, I checked the direction the breath was flowing from the nostrils, checking to see if there really was any connection between the moon and how the breath flowed, or the breath and anything else. Astonishingly, the connections between what the text explained and what happened in real life matched.

Each of the five elements of creation—earth, water, fire, air, and ether—had a time frame in which they flowed, and although the changes for me as a novice observer were different from what the text gave, there were changes indeed. This subtle science captivated me with its implications for doing postures and, most important to me, meditation. All the while all sorts of people would show up at the ashram with life situations as interesting as my practices.

Bhagavan, a fellow ashram denizen, motioned for me one afternoon from the tent's shade where he had been talking to a very earnest looking man for some time.

"Charles, you may want to talk to this man. He seems to be having trouble with his meditation practice."

Bhagavan's English was perfect, like Prem's, but his family hailed from Curacao. He often marveled at how well Carol and I got along.

"You know, I write home to people about you two."

"Why's that?"

"You're both so serious about your practice, and you live in such small quarters and have not killed each other? That's a wonder to me." Bhagavan's story might have been slightly different had he been a fly on the wall during some of the more heated discussions that we, like all couples, had.

"So, what's with this man? What kind of trouble is he having? I see you've been talking to him for some time."

"Well, it's not really trouble . . . I'll let him explain it to you. He seems to be beyond anything that I know about."

I walked to the area under the tent where Bhagavan and the man had been sitting.

"What seems to be the problem, sir?" I posed the question to the pleasant-looking Indian man with mixed gray hair sitting under the tent.

"You see," he said to me. "I'm having this problem with my meditation. Let me first tell you that I subsist only on *nimbu pani* (lemon water)," as he went on in his heavily Hindi accented English.

Whoa, if this is true, this man is already out of my league.

The man continued. "When I sit in mediation, it lasts for eight hours at a time. The problem is that when I'm sitting, I begin to tremble."

"Tremble? What do you mean tremble?" The man sat upright in his chair and opened his shirt to display his chest and abdomen area. As he sat there, lost in concentration in a moment's time, the right side of torso began this muscular twitching.

"Is this twitching I see what you are talking about?"

"Yes," the man said, and he rebuttoned his shirt. With this

demonstration, I am less impressed than before, but who was I to say this man didn't have something.

"Do you ever see visions of deities or anything?" I fully expected this man to say no and that would be the end of my enquiry. I'd suggest to him a relaxation exercise, not sit so long, or not sit and sleep, and he'd go away, unhappy, but he'd go away.

"Yes," the man said, "I see the deity all the time. When I sit, I see Shiva seated in meditation. He is as tall as the two-story building there."

Hey, I was seeing Shiva on hospital walls. Maybe this man is on to something.

Sure that Bhagavan's referral was like no one I'd ever talked to, I asked, "Sir, with your experiences . . . I'm sure that I can't help you. I suggest that you see Swamiji if you can."

The man was delighted at my suggestion. I had no idea what it would mean for him.

About an hour later I passed the man, looking frazzled and disturbed, scurrying out the back gate of the ashram that led out toward the Ganges. Prem was to come along shortly thereafter as I stood there wondering what happened with the man.

"Say, Prem, what happened with this man? He said he was seeing Shiva and sitting in deep meditation for hours on end. What did Swamiji have to say? He looked rather taxed as he left."

"Some people just can't bear to hear the truth. Swamiji tested his meditation, as only he could, and the man was just sitting sleeping, and all his visions were hallucinations from poor nourishment."

CHAPTER SIXTEEN

Living the Mystery

Certain places in and around Rishikesh were very special, and we were sent by taxi, with a note for the driver, on day trips to these places. One of these places was north of Rishikesh on the road to Badrinath and Kedarnath, holy shrines in the high Himalayas. Vasishtha Guha, the cave of Vasishtha, reputed to have been the place where the sage, the guru of Lord Rama, had done his practice. I loved these stories, there was something about them that was quaint, and comforting, the mythology of the real India.

After banging along the mountain roads in our Ambassador, the car of choice for taxis in India, we pulled off to the right side of the road. In the distance, we could see traces of the Ganges through the tops of trees and nothing else.

Our taxi driver, in his best English, said, "*Bhai* (Brother), the Vasishtha Guha, down." The Indians called me brother, and it made me feel right at home.

"Down?"

He pointed to a stairwell that could have been missed had it not been pointed out. Carol and I made our way toward the stairs and down the winding, angular staircase, first one direction, then another until we got to the bottom of the hill. The treetops that we saw from above had their origins in this little valley. On our left, as we moved toward the cave, was a long, one-story building that housed, if nothing else, the kitchen for the compound. The smoke from cooking blackened the cement as it escaped through the steel-bar-studded opening above the door of the room.

There were one or two swamis around, but they seemed uninterested in trying to extract money from us for *pujas*, unlike the priests at other shrines that we had visited. As we walked by these swamis in this pleasant little oasis between the dusty road and the Ganges, we headed toward the opening of the cave. A wooden façade had been built around the opening of the cave that served the purpose of housing a pictures of saints and traditional Vedic gods, all for sale.

There was no light in the cave that could be seen from the entrance, and I walked ahead of Carol as the scout for this adventure. As I crossed the threshold of the actual cave, beyond the wooden facade, I heard OOOOOOOMMMMMM.

I whispered to Carol, "Oh . . . I see they're playing this cave scene for all its worth."

"What do you mean?" she said, curiosity in her voice.

"You don't hear that?"

"Hear what?"

"Wait a minute, wait a minute let's . . . let's go back outside, you must've missed it."

We turned around in the entrance to the cave—we hadn't gone six feet into it, not nearly enough to actually see anything in the cave's darkened interior. We went back to the exterior of the cave, to the wooden façade that decorated its entrance.

Outside the cave, I asked her again, "Are you sure you didn't hear anything?"

"What was I supposed to hear?"

"You weren't supposed to hear anything. No, no . . . you were supposed to hear something. The sound they have set up that plays when you cross the threshold of the cave. You'll see what I mean. Let's go in again."

With that, we started in again. This time I walked cautiously ahead of Carol to see where they had the electric eye or whatever set off the sound in the cave. As we crossed the actual threshold of the cave, past the wooden façade, the sound was there again, OOOOOOOOOMMMMMMMM. The sound was only on my right side, in my right ear. I stopped, with Carol nearly bumping into me.

"Don't you hear that?" I whispered.

"Hear what?"

She didn't hear it, but it was there. I was experiencing it; it was captivating, and stayed with me as we found our way into the cave's darkened sanctum, where a small ghee lamp was the only light burning in an alcove. A few other people sat around the perimeter of the cave in the dark, meditating. I hoped we hadn't disturbed them with our comings and goings, and whispering.

We sat for a while on the floor of the cave to meditate, not really having come prepared, as we had no cushions to sit on or mats to protect our ankles. It made me wonder how the yogis who lived in these caves got along without sticky mats, zabutons, and cushions for their butts.

This place had a profound energy, and proved to me that stories about places like this had some validity. We spent a few hours in the cave's vicinity, down by the Ganges walking among stones smoothed by the running water, and we visited another, smaller cave at the back and outside the main cave. I went away from our day trip dumbstruck at what happened.

Not far from there, on a stony embankment of the Ganges, stood another little ashram, Jeevan Dhara Sadhana Kuttir, home to the Catholic nun Vandana Mataji. I had met her at the behest of a friend who, knowing my training as an interfaith minister, thought I might find her take on meditation and spiritual life interesting. We first met Mataji at a Syrian Coptic church service. Unlike any Christian service I had ever attended, it was all done in Hindi, right down to the hymns, none of which I was familiar with. I asked Mataji if she would allow me to interview her. She agreed, and atop the roof of her little ashram, overlooking the Ganges, I got the chance to ask her about the service and many other questions I had about her unique take on the spiritual life.

"Mataji, I could follow what was happening in the service by symbol and gesture, but I didn't follow the Hindi. My Hindi is not that good." Mataji laughed. She was a lovely little, golden-brown woman, in her seventies, who spoke the Queen's English, and had an extraordinary take on the religious life.

"You know, my love for Indian culture stems from my college days."

"What do you mean by that?"

"I was born into the Zoroastrian tradition, Parsi. There are also people in my family who are Theosophists, and when I was young, I would go to their meetings in Adyar and Varanasi."

"Your family was pretty open minded."

"Yes it was."

"So why are you a Catholic nun?" I now have astonishment on my face.

"That's a long story, but in a nutshell, it has to do with a few people who impressed me in the convent school I attended."

"You went to a convent school? I thought you said you were a Parsi at birth."

"Yes, but you know the Parsi religion is dying out. I grew up with my own Parsi culture, unlike some others who are straight away sent to convent schools, never learning their traditional culture."

"So what is so significant about doing a mass or any church service in Hindi, you being Catholic and also English speaking?"

In the little sanctuary of the ashram, I'd been impressed by the picture of Jesus sitting in *siddhasana* (a meditative posture). This gave me the feeling that I could ask Mataji many questions that I couldn't get answers to anywhere else.

She continued, "There was this idea among some of us that the church should reflect our culture. Sure there are those who felt that this means we want to Hindu-ize the church, but these people are misguided."

"What would be wrong with taking elements like yoga and adding them to the practices of Christianity?"

"Precisely, and this is something that we work to do here at our little interfaith ashram. You know, there have been priests who've come here with the most interesting question. They ask me why I think people are leaving the church?"

"I had something like this happen to me at home. The World

Council of Churches sent a party to our center in New York and asked us a similar question."

"What did they ask?"

"The leader of the party asked me why I thought people were leaving the church and seeking answers in places like ours. I told her my story of the pastor telling me that meditation was evil. That's why people were coming to us, and investigating Buddhism and other meditative traditions."

"Yes, this seems to be true. You are spot on with this."

"So Mataji are you a guru?"

She chuckled, "I'm more a guru in mind, some people might think of me this way. But you know, a real guru is God alive in human flesh. I don't see myself that way. Swami Sivananda was my example here. He said you can always be of assistance to someone who is newer than yourself on the path. In that way, I help."

"You knew Swami Sivananada?"

"No, I am a student of Swami Chidananda, the current head of the Divine Life Society. It is from him that I have learned about Swami Sivananda."

"How long have you known Swami Chidananda?"

"Every six months for six years we used to live at the ashram. We would then go back and give retreats at our community on what we learned."

"What'd your order think of this?"

"Well, they trusted us. I was in my forties by then and I already had three years experience at the ashram before we started giving the retreats. All of this was after a national conference where Swami Abhishiktananda started us off."

"Abhi . . . shikta . . . nanda? Abhishiktananda? I know that name. That was the name of the swami whose little book on prayer was lying on the vocation directors desk at Gethsemane. So this swami was a great influence on you?"

"From my perspective, this was no ordinary swami. Dom Henri Le Saux . . . "

"What do you mean Henri Le Saux?"

Mataji continued, "Swami Abhishiktananda came to India as Henri Le Saux, from the Benedictine tradition, with the attitude that India was pagan and filled with false gods and idols. He had the good fortune of meeting Ramana Maharshi, but he became the student of a little -known sage named Gnanananda."

"Now, I've heard of Ramana, my master teacher talks about him in his autobiography, *Living With The Himalayan Masters,* and I've studied Ramana's *Who am I.*"

"Your teacher is Swami Rama?"

"Yes ma'am, do you know him?"

"Yes," she said as she smiled. "He once asked me to oversee an ashram for him. Anyway, Abhishiktananda started us off in a sense."

"What do you mean by that?"

"For example, he wrote something that speaks about the conflict he noticed between his experience as a priest and his yearning for what the Indian sages teach. He has, in one of his diaries, asked the question, 'Should I seek peace in what is beyond the 'I', peace within?' He questioned if he, as a Christian, had a right to such peace."

"This going beyond the small 'I', the ego. That is what Vedanta teaches isn't it? This is what Ramana's experience was right?

"Yes, it is. I see that you are very familiar with the nuances of Indian philosophy."

I hadn't told her about my graduate work and my study of the seven systems of Indian philosophy. I had introduced myself as someone from *Yoga International* magazine. Swamiji had designated me as an international sales manager at the magazine's inception. I took it upon myself to interview her, thinking it might hold some interest for the magazine's readers.

"I'd like to read more about this man, can you recommend any reading"?

"Certainly, just read *The Secret of Arunachala: A Christian Hermit on Shiva's Mountain.*"

This man's struggle intrigued me. I could identify with his yearning for peace, but being in conflict with himself.

"So Mataji, you go about teaching this interfaith idea. Christianity doesn't have all the answers?"

"The real knowledge of the inner life, the knowledge that India has nurtured and preserved, seems lost to the Church. You know, I've spent time teaching meditation, and I teach it to Christians and Hindus alike."

"That's very interesting. Does that go over well here?"

"Something interesting happened when I spoke to a group in Bengal about this very thing. They were totally surprised by my presentation."

By now I understood that this little nun, as sweet as she seemed, wasn't above raising a few eyebrows.

"Bengal is known as a center of worship of the divine feminine," I said.

"Yes, and listen to what happened when I spoke there," she chuckled. "When I stood before the audience of nearly ten thousand people I began by chanting *Om Shakti Om Shakti Om*. The audience went wild." My eyes widened as I listened to Mataji's story.

"Were they offended, Mataji?" I said with surprise.

"No, they were enthralled, they . . . they were . . . flabbergasted that a Catholic nun stood before them and chanted a name of the divine mother, *Shakti*. That is the only time I've ever gotten a standing ovation."

I could see from her expression that this was a seminal event for Mataji, almost as important as having her little ashram by the Ganges.

"You know they didn't want us here, our little interfaith ashram?"

"Who didn't want you here, Mataji?"

"Oh, the powers that be here in the city. They said, 'Why should a Christian have an ashram here? What does she want?' Well, Swami Chidananda spoke up for us since we had lived at the ashram. So we have our little ashram here by the Ganges."

Mataji's duties forced us to end our meeting, but it was quite fruitful for me, and I left through the gates of her little ashram and headed for the streets of Laxman Jhula to get a *vikram* (taxi) back to Swami Ram ashram. It was a pleasant winter evening's walk, the last stretch of my return to the ashram, along the banks of the Ganges, marveling at the stars twinkling in her holy waters. It was Christmas Eve, no big day for the average Indian in Rishikesh.

CHAPTER SEVENTEEN

If You Like

New Years Eve brought a busload of Himalayan Institute Hospital Trust (HIHT) staff to the ashram. There was to be *satsang* (good company), *prasad* (blessed food), and kirtan (chanting), something I really enjoyed when it was done well. Swamiji had tweaked my interest in chanting, in Indian music in general, by having Saturday night chanting sessions at the Honesdale ashram. Some of the finest artists in the world performed for Swamiji at our ashram in Honesdale. Swamiji was a respectable musician himself and truly enjoyed it when the likes of Amjhad Ali Khan, the sarod master, or Pandit Jasraj, the master classical vocalist, performed for him and us.

"All right, someone lead a chant." Swamiji asked around the big open hall whose floor was covered with red hemp mats for carpeting. As soon as one chant ended, another person started up another.

"Hey, Charles, you should lead a chant," whispered Kamal as she nudged me in the side. Kamal had been one of my dishwashing partners at the ashram, and she'd heard me sing.

"Kamal, singing in the dish room and singing in front of people who really know what they are doing with chanting are two different things," I whispered.

"Oh, come on, you can do this." She had more confidence in this venture than I did. I was concerned about performing the genre properly.

"It would be like an opera singer trying to sing gospel or vice versa. The styles are different."

"What?" Kamal said, "Come on."

One chant ended after another, and Kamal kept elbowing me.

"Seee – taaaa Raaamm, Seee – taaaa Raaamm," came the words to one chant I'd heard Swamiji do, as I began singing sitting in the crowd somehow hoping to be heard, but not seen.

As soon as I began, Swamiji said, "Hey!"

I froze, sure now that listening to Kamal had gotten me in trouble, my actions having stirred my teacher to advise me to leave the singing to people who knew the genre.

"Come up here." Expecting the worst, I proceeded to the front, where he was sitting on the floor leaning on a red cushion.

"Sing." I was surprised and honored. One of my unspoken wishes was to sing for Swamiji, and here was my chance. The audience joined in the chanting of Sita Ram, and at least they didn't throw things. One of the engineers, a music connoisseur, spoke to me afterwards.

"You don't quite have the nuances of the genre, but you do have the soul."

His remarks gave me confidence, remarks that Kamal overheard and nodded an approving "I told you so."

Six months rolled by, and the time came when we had to leave the ashram because our tourist visas were going to expire. Carol and I were both saddened at the prospect of having to leave a difficult but rewarding lifestyle and return to the U.S. to find work. We'd both forgotten about my dream.

One sunny morning around the tent, I reminded Swamiji, "We will have to leave in a short while."

"Who said you have to leave?" he said, with the slightest bit of irritation in his voice.

"If we don't have to leave, then what do we do?"

Swamiji acted as if he didn't hear this, as he turned away and mounted the white SUV that daily took him to the hospital site. His hospital-assigned security guard entered after him and they drove away. I'd come to understand the need for security later our stay.

Carol and I stood there looking at each other with questioning eyes.

"What do we do about the information in the dream, Carol? Remember, he said that we wouldn't leave until after a year. What do we do?"

Swamiji left that very day we spoke to him and did not return to the ashram at all during our last weeks. The question of what to do plagued us to the last minute before leaving Sadhana Mandir.

We pestered Kamal on the balcony outside Swamiji's apartment, where she had a little room and an office where she was trans-creating a book with Swamiji.

"Kamal, what should we do? Swamiji's gone. Can you contact him to get some clarification about what we should do?"

"I'll see what I can do." After two days, Kamal got back to us.

"Charles, I asked Swamiji your question. Should you stay here or return to the U.S., and he said, 'If you like.'"

"If you like? What does 'if you like' mean? That's no answer to the question."

If anyone knew what cryptic responses like this meant it would be Kamal, but it was as much a mystery to her as it was to us.

She said, "That's all he said."

"All right, Carol, we tried our best to have a plan, to avoid chaos, but it's no use when it comes to Swamiji." Saying this out loud, my conscience chided me—Swamiji was not to blame on this. "We still have only succeeded in creating a drama."

Feeling that I should know what to do, and feeling disheartened at not trusting the dream instructions, brought my decision making to a halt.

Carol replied, "Well, I guess we should get our stuff together and order up a taxi. What do you think?"

"I guess that is the only conclusion to come to." Dismayed, the next day we loaded up our suitcases, souvenirs and all, and headed by taxi to New Delhi, not knowing if the government of India was going to allow us to return or not. We had no idea of what to expect.

"Carol, remember when we started, before even coming to India? Remember when we asked people how they fared in India, what they said?"

"In our supposed wisdom, we hadn't asked even one of them what they did in this situation."

"No . . . ," I said, "They'd told us without our asking, but we don't remember what they said. We have been here in Shangri-la and forgotten everything."

"At least we had the forethought before leaving New York to make arrangements to stay at Sharma's apartment in Delhi, if we needed to." When the drama started to unfold, we had contacted our friend to see how to proceed, just in case.

"Thank God for that, What did Sharma say we were supposed to do?"

Hearing this, Carol looked through her purse for her little note pad where we'd saved all our friend's instructions.

"I have it copied down here, hold on." The notepad that contained the instructions was difficult to locate bouncing around in the back of the Ambassador taxi, as we were. We had luggage in the trunk and all around us. The instructions read:

Go to apartment directly above Sharma's
and get the keys to the apartment. Just knock on the door
and introduce yourselves. They'll be expecting you.

"That's all it says? Well, I guess that's all it would need to say."

"Yep," Carol shrugged, "You gave the taxi driver the address, so we just have to sit back and ride."

And ride we did, never losing our sense of trepidation, and the Delhi police didn't help.

"Why are you pulling over here?" was my question to the taxi driver as we pulled over in the dimming evening light of New Delhi.

"Police."

"Police?"

Looking through the rear view mirror, I saw the policeman motion the driver to exit the car. After some talking, the driver returned to the taxi, rummaged through the glove box, and returned to the policeman with some yellowed papers. The policeman made his way to the taxi, opened the front passenger side door, stuck his head inside the car, and looked into the back seat at us.

"*Kase ho.*" I made no indication that I knew any Hindi. Although

I knew what he was saying, I wouldn't have been able to carry on an extensive conversation. Seeing what he could only take as a European woman and a not-quite Indian man, the policeman grunted and backed his way out of the car's passenger side door. The taxi driver returned shortly thereafter.

"So, what did the police want?"

"He say we don't have proper paper to drive in city. He want *bakshish* (a bribe), but I have no money."

Lucky we hadn't paid the driver for his services yet, so he didn't have any money to speak of, other than the necessary few rupees. It wasn't the first time we had run into *bakshish*.

Bedraggled and tired after our dusty, six-hour taxi ride, we finally found our way to Sharma's apartment complex. Unloading the taxi, we made our way to the elevator. After checking the location and number of our friend's apartment, we rolled our luggage back to the elevator and made our way to the floor above. Directly above where we were staying, we knocked on the ornate wooden door of the apartment.

"Carol, I just remembered something. Sharma said his apartment is just below the apartment that Swamiji uses." As I said this, Swamiji himself opened the door and asked us in. Carol and I stood there, wide-eyed.

Swamiji said, "Well, come in, come in."

"Swamiji, you are here?"

"So what are you two doing here?" *Didn't he know?*

"Swamiji we have to leave the country to get our visas renewed. We are staying in the apartment below, and needed to get the key, that's why we're here . . . at your door it seems."

"Yes, so you are staying in Sharma's apartment?"

"Yes, sir."

"Where will you go to get your visas?"

"We spoke with Victor, and thought we might go to Italy and renew our visas there. The law just requires that we leave the country and then come back in."

Victor, our German friend, had married an Italian woman, and they lived in the Tuscan area of Italy.

"Yes, Vickie was just at the ashram recently with his wife."

"Yes, sir, and he asked us to come to Florence to teach, so we thought we'd go there, teach, and get our visas renewed."

As for visas, Swamiji had travelled all over the world in service to his master and the tradition. He knew all the ins and outs of visas and passports.

"Why will you go so far just to renew your visas? Why not go to Nepal?"

"Nepal, is it nice there?"

"Oh, yes, you will like it there. We had an ashram there for a while, and were, for some time, in service to the royal family."

"How did that come about?"

"My master sent me there."

This was a story I wanted to hear more about, but Swamiji stopped there.

As we made our way to our friend's apartment Carol marveled, "It's lucky we ran into Swamiji. He had information that will save us time."

"Hmm, just the kind of stuff we were fretting about on the ride."

The next day, with the help of a local per diem tour guide we'd befriended at the ashram, we found our way to the visa offices in Delhi and got transit visas to Kathmandu, Nepal. Fourteen days later, after visiting Buddhist stupas and shrines, and watching the sunrise over the high Himalayas, we returned to Delhi, visas renewed, ready to continue our adventure. Upon returning to the ashram, we found there had been changes.

"Prem, it looks like someone was using our little bungalow."

Prem said, "We didn't know if you were really coming back, so while you were gone a few people did retreats in it."

"Oh," I said to Carol, "I'm surprised that we're so easily forgotten after staying here night and day for so many months, and feeling as if the ashram were home."

"I know what you mean."

These were our thoughts. The next day brought news of further change.

"Swamiji says that you are to move to the hospital."

"Move to the hospital? But we don't want to move to the hospital. We want to continue to do practice here at the ashram." This was our plea to Swamiji when he returned to the ashram that evening in the big, white SUV.

"Now it is time for you to do some *seva* (selfless work). Besides, it will be oppressively hot here in the summer months, and the mosquitoes will be unbearable."

Mosquitoes, unbearable, that got my attention. I hated mosquitoes. I had grown to develop these little welts when certain ones bit me. I had names for the two types that I saw around the ashram. There were these rather large ones with a dark grey thorax with light grey stripes around it, and then there were smaller brown ones. I called the big ones B-52 bombers, and the little ones P-51 Mustang fighter planes, both World War II model airplanes I had assembled when I was kid. The P-51s were the ones that caused me the most grief. Getting away from them was okay with me. Little did I know that the P-51s, unlike the B-52s, had a much wider range than just near the Ganges.

"Prem? How will we get to the hospital every day?"

"Well, you can take a taxi or you can take the bus. The bus is cheaper."

"About how much is the taxi from here to there?" The bus idea didn't sound so great.

"The bus is much cheaper, and unless you have unlimited rupees, the bus is your best bet."

"You have a point here. We have no idea how long we'll be here or how often we'll be commuting, so maybe the bus is our best bet."

We didn't have an unlimited source of rupees, exchanging travelers checks for rupees in Rishikesh was a nightmare at the time, and all the work we'd do at the hospital would be volunteer.

Still not wanting to move to the hospital, we'd take a bus from Rishikesh in the morning and ride the twenty-five-plus kilometers to the hospital. The signs on the buses weren't very useful, and the schedules weren't quite standardized, but some part of me found that intriguing.

"Carol, I'm pretty sure that the sign on the front of the bus says Dehra Dun."

"*Bhai, Dehra Dun?*" My best take on asking the bus driver if the bus was going to Dehra Dun. The hospital was between Rishikesh and Dehra Dun.

"*Nahi, Kedarnath.*" No, said the driver, the bus was going to Kedarnath.

I could read the Hindi script, but no matter, and this often happened, if the bus sign said Dehra Dun, the driver might say it was going somewhere entirely different. You always had to ask before you mounted the bus and paid your fare, and then there was always the language barrier—my Hindi was rudimentary. The Hindi script, with a few exceptions that always caught me, is the same as Sanskrit. We had studied the rudiments of Sanskrit in grad school.

After a time, the bus travel proved to be too much. Twenty-five kilometers by bus in the foothills of the Himalayas was not the same as moving about on a bus in Manhattan, or was it?

CHAPTER EIGHTEEN

The Hospital

"Do you think Swamiji knew this commute thing wasn't going to work out? He's probably just chuckling away."

Carol laughed as we loaded all our suitcases into the trunk of an Ambassador taxi and prepared to move our quarters to the hospital.

Our bungalow was to be at the single residents' quarters, so it was small—but luxurious compared to our ashram digs. Most important was that we had a place to cook, an unexpected pleasure. Local Indian cuisine was very, very good, but very, very hot.

Carol said, "Let's see, we have room for beds over here, and this part can be our front room and dining area."

I was looking around the bathroom. "Well, here you have your bathroom," sounding more like a realtor showing a home.

"Ah, yes, you have an excellent polished stone squatter with nearby chrome waterspout to wash your hinder parts after relieving yourself." Carol is rolling her eyes at my silliness.

"Here is your sink, and a shower." Bucket baths, with water you heated yourself, were still the order of the day. The water was heated with what amounted to an oversized tea cup water boiler. You only got water hot enough for a shower in the summertime when the black, rooftop tanks held water that was heated in the summer sun, and then you didn't want it.

After we settled in, we reported to our friend Dr. Bova.

"Here are your assignments," she said.

Barb was not only a department head at the hospital but a friend. She kept it to herself but she was a highly accomplished hatha yogini. She lived two doors over from us.

"Charles, you report to the Rehabilitation Department Head, and Carol, report to the Elementary School Head."

Both Carol and I were to teach doctors and med school students meditation and hatha yoga in addition to our assigned duties. Swamiji trusted us to do that—after all we had been doing that for years up to that point.

In the Rehab Department, I got to work with Dr. Rajesh, a lovely, tiny, older woman who had studied in the U.S. for many years, and was a student of Swamiji's.

"Charlie," a name that didn't sound bad coming from this lovely little Indian lady, "Swamiji has recommended that you work with me. What do you do that is unique?"

"Dr. Rajesh . . . hmmm, I've been trained as a counselor, but I'd find this difficult here with the language barrier."

"No, no . . . I mean something else unique. We had a colleague of yours here who was trained in Shiatsu. Swamiji hinted that you were good at massage."

"Oh, that must be because I have worked on his body just a little, but I have had no official training or certification in massage. I wouldn't feel comfortable working with people that way."

"So what shall we assign you to do?" Rajesh was a pleasant woman whose white coat always seemed too long to me; maybe that was because she was so tiny.

"Well, my graduate research revolved around using yoga to control hypertension and yoga therapy, and I have studied some energy healing methods."

"I'm interested in what you know about high blood pressure, but what are these so-called energy healing methods?"

"I have learned Reiki and Pranic Healing."

"How might we use those in our hospital setting? Can you train one of my people in this sort of thing?"

"I'm not really sure," I was hesitant about teaching Reiki even though I was trained to, and the Pranic Healing was too involved.

"I don't know how that would work in this setting."

"What do you do with all this anyway?"

"Well, you sort of put your hands on different parts of the body and pass energy, prana, to those places to help in the healing process."

"Let's see what it is. I will send you a few patients."

"Hey, Dr. Rajesh, remember my Hindi is virtually nonexistent."

That would change somewhat over the course of the year, although, the language issue was not my primary concern. I couldn't put my finger on why I was so hesitant about this suggestion.

"I'll assign you a Hindi-speaking assistant, you'll be okay."

"All right . . . ?" My gut was telling me that this was going to be trouble, but I didn't listen. The regular treatment room was a big space with several observation tables, reflexology charts on the wall, and other medical equipment on the tables. I was sent patients with ailments like cervical spondylitis (a stiffening of the vertebral column), scoliosis, and hypertension. Over the course of a few days, I worked with several patients with yoga therapy, but only one using the energy work, after which the word came.

Rajesh walked into the little office I was using for the hypertension research with its observation table, desk, biofeedback equipment, blood pressure cuff, and barely enough room to teach people a few postures.

"Charlie, Swamiji says you must stop doing the energy work."

"I thought this might happen; it sort of felt awkward for some reason."

"When I told him what I had you doing, he said, 'Why is he doing such things? He should just be doing yoga therapy,' so we must stop."

"What else did he say?"

"Well, since we want to establish the hospital as a force in the surrounding area, and in the country, Swamiji said we shouldn't do such esoteric things. The medical establishment won't understand."

"That's more than fine with me, but I would like to show you something about this type of work that's interesting." It felt like a burden had been lifted off my shoulders.

"Okay?"

"We need a new patient from your file, someone that I have not met." Rajesh and I walked back to her office. She sat behind her desk, and I sat down in one of the several chairs in her curiously spacious little office.

"Here you go." She'd found what she thought was an appropriate patient and began to explain to me his diagnosis. I stopped her.

"No, don't tell me the patient's diagnosis, just give me the person's name and age." She told me the young boy's name and age, and looked at me, puzzled.

"Okay, give me a while' and I will come back and tell you what I find, and how we can help him."

"You what?" she said with an incredulous expression.

"Yeah, yeah I know, just let's see if what I get makes any sense. You have nothing to lose by this experiment right?"

"That's true."

A day or so later I returned to Rajesh's office with my findings.

"Dr. Rajesh, here is what I got from my screening." Rajesh looked at me with an open but questioning expression.

"The boy seems to be fine from his chest up, but there seems to be something amiss below his solar plexus." I pointed to the level from the child's navel and below on the little diagram I had drawn.

Rajesh looked a little bewildered, "I have only given you this patient's name, and you think that from his navel down there is a problem?"

"Well, Dr. Rajesh, I said that it was just a little experiment with something I had learned. I wasn't expecting huge results."

Her eyes widened a bit, "The boy has muscular dystrophy. You haven't come up with the exact disorder, but you certainly have uncovered where he has most been affected by his condition. How did you know this, and what would you do about it?"

How I came to the conclusions about the boy was a mystery even to me. It was all about what appeared to be simple movement of the hands in space. I had gotten the results from the energy work just as clearly as if I had met the boy in person, but I needed to talk to Dr. Barb about how to approach working therapeutically with the child. I had never worked with anyone with such a serious condition using yoga therapy.

As I walked through the whitewashed halls of the hospital, I thought about how I would go about providing yoga therapy for the boy. I knew all sorts of advanced practices with fancy names that I thought might help like *mayurasna* (peacock) and *agni sara* (fire essence), both directed at increasing the healing fire in the solar plexus, but I also knew that these things were only therapeutic if a person had some facility with them. As I got close to Dr. Barb's office, she appeared in the hall, smiling, as we met.

"So, Dr. Barb, I have a child with muscular dystrophy, how should we approach treating him?"

"Charles, remember all the yoga therapy you learned and practiced in grad school?"

Barb had been on staff during my grad school days, giving seminars, and amazing everyone with how adept she was at hatha yoga.

"Yeah, and it's proven helpful here in the Rehab department. The simplest things produce the most profound effects. It's fascinating to watch."

"Good, then think about the simple postures you would do for someone who had problems with their lumbar area, lower back, and legs. What breathing practices would you have them practice?"

"Hmmm, okay, I see."

She had given sage advice that only someone with her background could give. I saw the little boy a few times, and he was sent home to practice what I taught him with his parents' assistance.

Things like this happened often during our service at the hospital, and many times the results were quick and obvious. None more so than one little lady, sent to me after she was diagnosed with hypertension.

The woman, the denizen of a local village, came in to see me with her husband. As she approached me, she saw the observation table and the EMG, a biofeedback machine, with its blinking lights and wires hanging from it.

She said, "*Chelo* (let's go, let's leave)," as she turned and grabbed her husband's arm and headed for the door.

"*Mem Sah'b, Mem Sah'b* (Ma'am, Ma'am)."

I caught her attention before she had completely bolted, and with the help of my interpreter, I showed her that the equipment wasn't going to cause her any pain by hooking myself up to it. With the aid of my interpreter, we taught her breathing and relaxation exercises. I was getting a chance to follow up on the things I learned doing my master's research on a live population.

I had tried many experiments with breathing, some related to the work with hypertension, and some not.

"Tell me again, what you're doing?" These were Swamiji's words after I explained to him the practice I had undertaken on my own.

Rather hesitantly I said, "Okay . . . I began just doing *kapalabhati,* then *bhastrika,* and then I would just hold my breath for as long as I could."

"So that is no problem. Are you staying within your capacity?"

"I think, but that's just it."

"What do you mean?"

"Well, the retentions started out simply, first one, then two minutes. That would be normal."

Awaiting reprimand at any moment, I continued my explanation.

"Then the retentions started to last, comfortably, for three or four minutes, and I started to think that I wasn't keeping time well, or doing the locks properly."

"Were you?" Swamiji glanced over my head, as if studying something. I showed him my chin lock and stomach lift (lock), and asked about my root and tongue locks.

"I got a more precise timer so I could be sure about the time, but became concerned when the retention time passed six minutes and headed toward seven."

"Why did you worry? Did you feel uncomfortable?"

"No, sir. I asked the doctors how long the brain could be without oxygen before there were problems. They told me that it's usually five to six minutes for a normal person. So I thought I should check with you. You are the only person I know who could advise me."

"It's okay," he said.

The peace and sense of well-being that the practice produced was well worth the effort. The only drawback to it was the amount of time, effort, dietary restrictions, and preparation necessary to maintain that sense of peace, something that just wasn't practical for a person in the work-a-day world.

The effects of such a practice were profound, but the patients didn't have any preparation for such things. An easy intervention that produced a simple but profound effect was just conscious awareness of breathing and relaxation. We sent the little lady home to practice just that, and suggested she return for two more sessions. I assumed I'd never see her or her husband again.

The next week, on the same day and at the same time, the little lady showed up at the Rehab department office.

"Dr. Rajesh, I see that the little lady has come back."

"Yes, when she talked with me originally, she said she didn't want to have to deal with doctors, and she didn't want to take medicine. She was adamant about it, so I knew she'd be a good candidate for what you're doing."

"We'll take her blood pressure before and after our session, but what were her original readings last week?"

"That's very interesting, Charlie, her blood pressure when she showed up in my office was 160/95, but after working with you it was lower."

"Okay, let's see what happens today."

The patient followed me to the treatment room, where I took her baseline blood pressure. Again, we went through our little routine with the help of the interpreter.

At the end of our routine, I said to her, "*Mem Sahib, Ap* practice?"

The interpreter, admiring my attempts, in Hindi, at urging the patient to practice, took over and reminded her to practice at home three times a day. Her blood pressure was much lower than when we started the session.

With a cheerful, "*Dhayavad* (thank you)," the patient left with her husband. When she came the third week, her blood pressure was in the normal range, and we just reinforced her practices.

"Now you go home and continue practicing what he has taught you," said Rajesh in Hindi, "and you won't have to come back to the hospital with this complaint." The little village woman was as happy as a lark—she was a quick study.

"*Namskar Doc Sah'b.*" The little lady, palms together, directed her words to Rajesh and then glanced at me. I responded to her with palms together, a gesture used for both greeting and parting, bidding her goodbye. These were the good days at HIHT.

Our mornings were filled with regular work at the hospital and at the school. At the hospital, we saw classrooms full of aspiring doctors, mischievous boys and well-mannered girls. We taught them everything from hatha yoga, and the psychophysiology related to it, to meditation. Some students, barely able to converse in English, could read and comprehend medicine and science books without a problem. One conversation with a group of students one morning reflected just how humorous our teacher–student interactions were for me.

"Sir," three boys stopped me on the road on campus, "We have a problem in class."

"Boys, remember, I told you at the beginning of our lectures that if you didn't understand the content, or I was speaking English too fast, stop me and we'd go over whatever it was."

"Yes, sir, but that is not the problem."

They understand the subject, I'm not talking too fast. So what?

"Sir," one of the boys said straightforwardly, "You don't speak proper English; that is the problem."

It took everything in me not to burst out laughing at the student's assessment of my English. Of course, those schooled in the vernacular of the Queen's English would think my American-ese, as Swamiji called it, a bit low brow. I tried my best to be more mindful of my word selection, but word selection or no, I never quite met the Queen's standard.

This type of thing made up most of our worries at the hospital, and this was no worry at all. We shopped locally for our food, haggled, with my poor Hindi, for vegetables at *Choi Pulia* (thieve's bridge) market, cooked our meals, and had plenty of time to do our hatha yoga, meditation and other practices.

One morning after I reported to work, Dr. Rajesh asked if I was interested in a new project.

"Charlie, would you like to work with a disciple of Ananadamayi Ma, a swami?"

"A swami who knew Anandamayi Ma, really?" We had been introduced to Anandamayi Ma, a most extraordinary woman saint of India, in Swamiji's autobiography, but we had never met her.

In a corner of Rajesh's office sat a woman, just listening to the excitement in my voice. I didn't know her, and Rajesh didn't think it necessary to introduce me to her at the time.

"What I want you to do is work with him on breathing. He is an old swami that this lady has brought here to the hospital."

"Breathing? Dr. Rajesh, this disciple of Ananadamayi Ma, this old swami needs help with breathing? Why would he need training in breathing?"

"Yes, breathing. You go to his room and see him and help him if you can with his breathing."

"All right . . . " My voice fully registered my confusion, but my excitement about meeting a true disciple of this saint drove me on. I arrived at his room, stepped across the doors threshold, and entered a strange environment. I had been a patient in a room just like this, but my room had not been aglow with the ochre color of renunciation.

The swami's ochre robes were on the vacant bed next to him, and a young attendant sat on the floor, dressed from head to toe in ochre robes, but the entire room was aglow with this color. I checked my vision by closing my eyes and opening them, but the room's hue didn't change. I moved to the bedside of the swami on his right side, his attendant sitting close by the head of the bed.

"Sir, how are you? I have been sent to help you with your breathing." Somehow I doubted that he understood my English.

Why has Rajesh sent me on this assignment?

The old swami, with his labored breathing, and in some distress on every exhalation, was saying something. I put my ear close to his mouth so I could hear what he was saying.

"Hey Ma," he'd inhale then again, "Hey Ma," as he exhaled, came the words repeatedly from the old swami's mouth. It sounded as if he was calling on Anandamayi Ma in his hour of need. I didn't know what to say. What good was I in the face of this man's devotion and faith in this saint?

"Sir, do you feel like you can work with your breath?" I was feeling my uselessness, but to my surprise, he motioned me to come closer so that I could hear more clearly what else he wanted me to hear.

"Opi . . . uh . . . "

"I'm sorry sir, what are you saying?"

"Opi . . . uh . . . m."

"Opium? Are you asking for opium, sir?"

He nodded his confirmation. Breathing wasn't what he needed, it was a doctor. He was in severe pain. I reported my concern to Dr. Rajesh.

Carol and I met in the hospital lobby for lunch, and I told her about my meeting with the disciple of Anandamayi Ma.

"Did you learn anything?" Carol said. As we walked toward the exits, and before I could say anything, the woman who had been sitting in Rajesh's office came up to us. With palms together, we greeted her.

"Yes, ma'am. You are the lady who brought the old swami in. You were in Rajesh's office."

"Yes, that was me." I was so glad she spoke English.

She asked, "What did you find out with the swami?"

"Well, ma'am, he was just repeating the name of Ma. Oh, and he asked for opium, so I reported that to Dr. Rajesh."

"Do you have a minute?"

I looked to Carol for an okay, it was lunchtime. She was just as curious as I was. "Surely, let's find a place to sit."

In the spacious lobby of the hospital, stairs semi-circled around from the first to the second floor, where there was a mezzanine, and in the corner was a bench.

"Would you like to know how the swami has come to be here?"

Carol and I both chimed in, "Sure."

"I had a dream. Anandamayi Ma came to me in a dream. She said, 'Go to the jungle, get my child, and take him to the Himalayan Institute hospital,' and this is what I have done."

"Did Swamiji see him yet, what did he say?"

"I spoke with the medical director. It seems your Swamiji and the medical director, Dr. Shobha, visited my swami. While standing at the end of the bed, the medical director said your Swamiji never looked more than once at my sick swami. He kept looking above the bed on the wall in front of them as she read from his chart. He seemed to be responding to something or someone over the bed. 'Yes,' he said at one point, 'It will all be taken care of'. Your Swamiji and the medical director then left the room."

With that, the lady whose name we never knew was done, and her thoughts trailed off to reverie, and we took our leave of her. Carol and went away wondering why the woman had confided in us, and wondering the meaning of it all. The day after test results showed that the nameless old swami had tuberculosis, and directions were to cease working with him because his condition was in the infectious stage. Bumping into the old swami's friend by chance in the hallway, she hurriedly expressed her latest news.

"I had another dream last night." She said. "This time Ma said, 'Hurry, take my child back to the jungle ashram. He must leave his body at the ashram.' I am hurrying to make arrangements, with your Swamiji's permission, to get my swami back to the ashram."

Not many hours later the old swami sped away in a hospital ambulance, back to his jungle ashram home where, we were told, he left his body shortly thereafter.

Our working days had the occasional events like this, or more often than not things like marauding monkeys atop Carol's classroom buildings or the occasional cobra taking a wrong turn into a preschool classroom. Our evenings at the hospital were just as pleasant as being at the ashram. After the sun went down, we'd walk the beautiful campus and often bump into Swamiji.

"Hey, Charles and Carol, come and walk with me," a voice came from across the median of flowers.

The green belt was the median for the main roads of the campus. In that median were countless varieties of plants, everything from mango trees to the beautiful and fragrant night queen, whose blossoms dispersed their fragrance more at night, a fragrance that was both captivating and overpowering.

Carol and I met up with Swamiji at a break in the median, and joined him and his attendant, one of the gate guards, for the evenings walk.

"Namaskar-ji," we both greeted Swamiji with the colloquial hello.

"How are you two doing this evening?"

"We're fine, sir," Carol chimed in.

As we walked along, Swamiji pointed and said, "Charles, you two," speaking to the guard as well, "Go over there and pull up those weeds. They are American weeds."

We'd just walked pass the main entrance to the hospital building, walking on what I still considered the wrong side of the road. It took some getting used to, the "left of way" being standard in India, just like in England.

This was a rather strange request.

"Swamiji, what do you mean that these are American weeds?" I assumed that seeds had traveled on the clothes or in the luggage of Americans and fallen in the open space between the main hospital building and the single residents building that we lived in.

"Do you see that weed over there," and he pointed. "Go and pull that weed, it is an American weed."

I picked out the weed he was pointing to, making sure not to make the same mistake I'd made earlier. During a period of over-exuberance at the ashram I'd decided to pull weeds to keep myself busy when I had no further capacity to practice meditation or do hatha yoga. One morning a guard at the ashram took more than a passing interest in what I was doing. In a flurry, and with his best English, the guard came running.

"What are you doing *bhai* (brother)? Stop that."

Very proud, flaunting my misguided spirit of service, dirt falling from the roots of the plant I held, I said, "Why, I'm pulling up the weeds around the edge of the sidewalk to help the ashram look nice." The gardener was on vacation, and I thought I was being helpful.

"*Nahi* (No), you must stop. You're pulling up flowers, not weeds!" I was pulling up the first shoots of the beautiful marigolds that adorned the ashram grounds. I'd never seen marigolds except in full bloom.

Still, not being too keen to pull up so-called weeds, I waited for the attendant to go first. When he grasped the weed in question, I followed suit with a similar weed. The attendant was able to pull his weed right up root and all. I struggled with mine.

His weed must have been in sandy soil. Hmm, there is no sandy soil around here.

I struggled a bit longer, with only grass stains on my hands to show for it. That weed had a firm resolution to stay in the ground. The attendant walked back to Swamiji, standing near Carol, and showed him the weed he'd pulled.

Swamiji examined it carefully and said, "Come on, Charles, let's keep walking,"

Can't go yet, I have to get this American weed out. There's something going on here. Why can't I pull up this weed?

I ran along to continue walking, puzzled by the course of events. After taking leave of Swamiji at his residence, Carol and I made our way around the green belt one more time.

"I'm going to go home now," Carol said, "We've walked a lot more than we usually do."

"I'm not going in yet, I have to go and pull this weed up. There's something I'm supposed to learn here. This is some sort of koan, some weird thing that Swamiji is trying to get me to understand."

"All right, suit yourself," my wife said with a chuckle and a smirk on her face as she strolled toward our apartment.

Construction was continually going on at the campus, so a three-foot long piece of rebar was easy to come by without much of a detour on my way back to that weed. So I set to work as the evening sky began to lose sunlight.

This was by far the most difficult weed I have ever come across.

After an hour of sweating, digging around the root with the

piece of rebar, getting puzzled looks from passersby, I finally got to the bottom tip of the root. When I finished my task I headed down the green belt to Swamiji's quarters.

Luckily, Swamiji was still available. There weren't any engineers or hospital administrators or doctors with him clearing up details about construction or service to patients.

"Swamiji," sweat rolling down my back, the heat and humidity of summer in India having taken its toll, "I got that American weed up. I knew I had to pull it up for some reason. I didn't break the root either." Somehow, I knew this was important.

Swamiji chuckled. "So you pulled the weed up did you?"

"Yes, sir, and here is the proof." I didn't know what kind of weed it was. I'd never seen any such weed in the U.S. "I couldn't help from breaking the little tendrils though."

He continued smiling, "It is only right, you can never get rid of America. Now go home and rest so you don't miss your meditation time in the morning."

Puzzled still, I took Swamiji's leave and headed back up the road. *What does he mean you can never get rid of America?* I'd eventually get what he meant—the time was fast approaching to renew our visas.

The next morning after our practice, Carol quizzed me, "We need to use these airline tickets we purchased or we are going to lose them."

She was right. We had extended the tickets as long as the airline would allow, and now it was use them or lose the return fare. We decided to ask Swamiji about it. We caught up with him walking the green belt that evening.

"Swamiji, if we don't use the airline tickets we have, we are going to lose the money we paid for them."

"So what?" and he turned his back and walked away, leaving us standing there in a quandary.

"So what? What does he mean, so what?" This wasn't something you could run after him and ask questions about. You wouldn't get a clear answer anyway.

"Well, I guess that means that we just have to forget about the tickets. Our time isn't up yet," Carol said.

"Can we afford to throw away fifteen hundred dollars?" I asked her. "I mean, we have been in India volunteering from the beginning. What did another fifteen hundred dollars mean in the great cosmic scheme of things, right?"

We made our way back to the apartment for our evening practice and then to bed.

"I will tell you when it is time to go." Swamiji's words bubbled up from my unconscious.

It was hours before dawn as Carol and I settled ourselves in our meditation positions for the morning's practice. Aside from my briefs, I covered myself with a shawl from head to foot to keep the mosquitoes at bay. There was something about the sheer ochre colored shawl, with the words *Sri Ram, Jai Ram, Jai Jai Ram,* written on it in Sanskrit, that I really liked.

The ceiling fan, our savior, not only from the heat but also from marauding mosquitoes, was whirling away. After my period of quiet sitting, guru mantra whirling in my head, I picked up my trusty Rudraksha mala and began the *Maha Mrtanjaya:*

Om Trayambakam yajamahe
Sugandim pusthi vardhanam
Urvarukamiva bandhanan
Mrityor mukshiya mamritat

During one of those evening lectures at the Hotel Ganga Kinare, when we had first arrived in India, Swamiji had mentioned this famous mantra. I questioned him about it when we arrived at the hospital.

"Two point four million repetitions of this mantra will eliminate the fear of death," he said.

"If you eliminate the fear of death, that means you have overcome attraction and aversion, and the sense of I-ness, basically freeing yourself of ignorance, if the yoga sutras are right."

"Yes, the yoga sutras are accurate in this respect."

"Can a mantra really eliminate the fear of death, sir?"

"What did I say?"

And with that I asked him to give us the practice to achieve one of my much yearned-for goals—freedom from the fear of dying, something that was necessary to be able to leave the body consciously.

The vibratory pattern the words made flashed through my mind as I sat there. Little did I know that the prayers' final request— help me be free from death and unite with immortality—was something I might need imminently.

A loud explosion physically jarred Carol and me in our meditation seats and interrupted all my passing wonder about *Mritanjaya*. Both Carol and I were hesitant to move to the window, although we could see the glow on our wall from the blazing fire across the nearby field.

I eased up toward the window, and through the curtain, in the distance, I could see flames leaping out of the jaws that were the chained gates of the helicopter hanger, smoke and flames racing into the predawn sky.

"What do you see?"

"Whoa! The helicopter's hanger is on fire."

Carol's eyes wide now, the news startling her more than the explosion.

"It appears that even here on these grounds, politics has a say in things."

"What do you mean, politics?"

"Remember the day the medical school opened? Remember all the protestors who showed up at the big tent?" There had been protests at the celebration of the hospital's opening. Protests that we as outsiders didn't really understand. Swamiji had spent a lot of time convincing the local people that the project was going to be good for the community.

"Yeah."

"Somebody did not get their way, so this has happened."

I wasn't far off in my summation. The local politicians' attempts to subvert the good work that was going on at the hospital had led them to make all sorts of outlandish claims. At one point, an article in the local paper surfaced that reported a hospital official was murdered. He was really on vacation. Much more palpable than the character assassination of the hospital project was a direct and violent attack on the hanger. Carol and I took a walk to the hanger that afternoon.

"Look ,Carol, you can see here where the chain was cut."

"Why would someone do this?"

"You know," I said, "this chopper was donated by someone to carry people out of mountain villages in an emergency." Carol looked sad. I was irritated. The chopper looked like a dragonfly, gutted by fire.

This didn't slow down the progress at the hospital; on the contrary, the buildings seemed to go up faster than ever. The chopper was insured, and aside from being an inconvenience, the corrupt politicians hadn't won out.

With things like this happening, the time passed quickly. In September 1995, another tour was coming through just like the one we had started with a year earlier. This trip was going to Varanasi, the city of lights, also known as Benares, or Kashi.

"Swamiji, is it all right if we go to Varanasi, if the tour has space for us?"

"Sure, why not," was the simple response.

"It's not as polluted as Delhi is it? On our last trip to get visas I contracted a lung infection from the air pollution in Kathmandu and Delhi. I don't want to go to another place where the petro-chemical in the air can be tasted in your mouth after a while.

"No, no, it's just fine there. You should go."

Going was easier said than done. The buses were full, there was no room for us. As destiny would have it, Swamiji had arranged for a couple to take a side trip to Tarkeshwar, and that left room for a couple, Carol and I, to go on to Varanasi.

Varanasi is a wonder, not just because of the sacred tantric shrines, like the one for Batuka Bhairav, the baby Shiva, but because of the energy the city exudes is overwhelming. The first night in our Best Western hotel, I sat turning my mala, going through my mental repetition.

Om Tryambakum yajamahe... Something curious was happening, or was it just my imagination? The next morning at 4:30 a.m. after my meditation, I returned to my mala and the repetitions. This time there was no mistake.

"Carol," I asked my wife later, "Did you notice anything?" This had come to be my standard quiz for her, and she knew I was on to something.

"Yeah, the mantra, *Mritanjaya*, it goes faster here."

"Kiddo, we are in a hotel, a Best Western hotel. God knows what has gone on in this room. The mantra doesn't just go faster, it goes faster than at the hospital or even at the ashram."

"It must be this city?"

"It is. It's Varanasi itself, I think."

Varanasi continued to enrapture us. One of our pilgrimage sites was Sarnath, the location of the Buddha's first sermon. As I stood on the walkway leading up to the little temple, tears welled up in my eyes. The famous stupa that stands on the very site where the Buddha delivered his famous first message peeked out between the palm trees, just like in the pictures I'd seen in my books.

What were the odds that I'd make it to this place in my lifetime?

A tear rolled down my face. I brushed it away and caught up to my wife entering the temple. The mystery of the mantra and walking in the footsteps of the Buddha were the highlights of Varanasi. Shortly thereafter, we took our leave of the tour, they headed to the states, and we returned to our duties at the hospital.

CHAPTER NINETEEN

Now It's Time to Say Goodbye

"You two people should go now. If you don't go you will be worthless."

These were Baba's words, New Year's Eve 1995. We had become acclimated to our environment and had picked up the usage of the name Baba, a word of affection meaning father, from our Indian guru brothers and sisters.

There was wisdom in his declaration. It would be very difficult fitting back into American society, and the regular workaday world in general, after having had so much time for what was really a retreat from the world.

Aside from that, it was obvious to everyone that something was changing in our teacher. We couldn't know just how little precious time we had left to be with him. On that clear December night, I asked him about his health and one special practice he had assigned to us.

"Baba, how long should we keep up the one special practice that you gave us?"

I was surprised when he gave me his answer, "You will continue this practice until I leave my body." In this was a vital clue. He immediately modified his statement and said, "No, you will continue this until one of us leaves our body."

There were rumors going around the campus. Some said that Baba was going to retire and return to his beloved Himalayan cave. To one individual, he declared that one day, November 13, he was going to just walk out. On that December night, it was obvious that he'd lost a considerable amount of weight, and he was coughing up big slugs of green phlegm and spitting it into a container. It was then I had an intense feeling and I asked him about it.

"Baba, will we ever see you again in this body that sits before us?"

I could tell this was another one of those questions he thought was either inappropriate for my level of understanding, or that I just had no business knowing the answer. He didn't answer me.

"Baba, will we ever see you again in this body?" I didn't know when he was going to leave his body, but I was certain it was going to be soon and that I would never see him again after we left the hospital. My mind questioned whether I was solid enough in my practice to no longer need a teacher.

"If you come back before one year, you will see me in this body."

I didn't know how literally true those words were. Our time to physically be with our teacher, while he was in a body, now numbered in days.

It was in the predawn darkness that we loaded up our taxi and headed again to New Delhi, this time for the last time. We had bid our friends and students farewell over the course of many painful days. As we loaded up, we were still puzzling over how we would settle our travel arrangements. We made our way to Sharma's apartment, and, again, with the aid of our trusty per diem guide, found all the necessary offices to make our arrangements.

For some strange reason, Baba urged us to check with the Delta office before buying our return tickets. At the Delta office, we were met with the unexpected. The office had officially closed, but the remaining skeleton staff's office manager looked at our documents.

"It seems these tickets, with their extensions, have expired . . . "

I cut her off, being unnecessarily impatient, "Yes, we know this. We just want to get tickets back to the states."

"Well, hold on a minute, let me check something." The manager walked to another section of the office and returned ten minutes later.

"Mr. and Mrs. Crenshaw, here is what I found."

Carol and I both looked at each other, expectantly, as the manager continued.

She said, "As you already know, Delta does not fly out of Delhi anymore, so it seems that you are entitled to have your entire fare returned."

We looked at each other in utter amazement.

"So that's about fifteen hundred dollars that we will have a credit for, right?" I asked.

"No, no," the manager went on, "What will be credited to your credit card account is thirty-eight hundred dollars."

"Thirty-eight hundred dollars?" I responded quizzically.

"Yes, that is what you're entitled to."

"Why, that's the cost of two round trip tickets, and the fees we paid for the extensions."

"I don't know exactly what the total is associated with, I can find out specifically if you wish, but that will take some time that I don't really have. I can tell you that this is what will be credited to you, as soon as you give me the account information."

After giving the manager our information, we got up, our eyes rolling in our heads over what we'd just heard, and as soon as we were outside the building, we looked at each other and said, "So what?!" simultaneously, laughing like teenagers.

It was our good fortune that, just as before, Swamiji turned up in his apartment above us in New Delhi and we got a chance to get some last-minute instructions for our journey, and the rest of our lives. With his blessings, we were off to the U.S., by way of Florence Italy, where we would present a few seminars, before we eventually landed at the Honesdale ashram.

"Go back to the U.S. and continue your teaching. Go, and they will help you." These were both comforting and confusing words coming from our teacher.

"So, Swamiji, we'll go to Honesdale for a while before moving on."

"What will you do in Honesdale?'

"We'll help Panditji."

His stern response was, "Don't stay there long," but then he continued in a tender tone, "Don't worry. I have all the plans."

Okay, plans now, you have all the plans. When do we get to see these plans? What are the plans? Where are the plans now? WHO is they?

These questions went unanswered, as his words, *"Jao, Jao"* (go–go) ushered me away from my thoughts before I could formulate them into a question.

Finding ourselves at the Honesdale ashram, unsure where we should go to begin our work or when we should leave, we looked at prospective sites, and considered returning to New York City.

"Charles, why don't we just stay here?"

"Panditji has said we are welcome to stay. The institute can always use help. The only problem is that Swamiji said not to stay here a long time. I don't understand why we can't stay here, but I know we can't stay." My wife heard the frustration in my voice; she was just as perplexed.

We knew that it was all going to boil down to us making our own decision. Wherever we were "sent" that wasn't our choice would be a source of dissatisfaction on some level. The plot thickened after November 1996.

Pandit Rajmani was leading a tour to India in September 1996. If we had been financially prepared to go, we would have proved Swamiji's prediction accurate. Less than two months after the tour embarked, on November 13, our master teacher left his body.

"You know, Carol, I have no idea who this old man who graced our lives was."

"Did they say what he died from, or how he died?'

"I haven't heard yet, but there is a prerequisite in the tradition that masters leave their body consciously, with witnesses to verify this fact."

"Riggghhht. Swamiji had witnessed the transition of many sages in his lifetime, including his master," Carol acknowledged

"You know, one of my fondest dreams, something I never told anyone, was to be present when Swamiji consciously withdrew from his body, but it obviously wasn't my karma. Do you think he really had the knowledge of how to move between life and death consciously and gracefully?"

"The only way to know is to speak with Kamal."

Many years before Swamiji had been near death. When he came to the U.S. that year, he spoke to us about how his body was failing.

"I may just have to drop this body in the forest in the high Himalayas." This caused an uproar in the ashram.

I remember saying a prayer under my breath, "Lord, you have led me to this master, now can you please not take him away just yet?"

Swamiji was gone from the United States for some time, and upon returning gave us some bittersweet news. He had asked his master, Bengali Baba, a vital question.

"Master, what will happen, what will it look like to the students if I die from such an injury?" As he was explaining this story, he stood before us, a picture of health.

With great sadness, he said, "My master's response was to give me his remaining years, his remaining life force, and to leave his body."

He continued talking and even stated how many years of *prana* he had received. To those who could hear beyond their astonishment, it was an indication of just what we were experiencing in November 1996. Whatever the truth of it, we had seen Swamiji rebound from what seemed to be the jaws of death before, but not this time.

I eventually was able to get in touch with our friend, guru sister, and Swamiji's longtime secretary and aide, Kamal, when she happened to be in the U.S. on family business.

"Kamal, can you tell me what happened when Swamiji left his body? I want to know the exact circumstances of him leaving his body. I know the tradition has specific guidelines for how someone with complete mastery leaves their body."

From my years of study, I knew about sages consciously leaving the body, and hoped that my own meditation practice would lead me to such level of mastery, if this phenomenon was real.

Kamal started, "The tradition says witnesses are required to validate how a master leaves his body. This is so that the tradition of consciously casting off the body continues."

"Yes, yes, I know, so were there suitable witnesses?"

"Yep, among the witnesses were people you know, Doctors Ganasan, Mohan Swami, and Barb Bova to name a few. The names of all the witnesses and how he left were recorded and sent to the cave monastery."

"I guess, scientifically, the doctors were important when it comes to the process of dying." Kamal continued, giving me a blow-by-blow account of our guru's departure.

"Baba was very weak those last days. On the evening of November 13, close to the time that he left his body, he kept looking at his watch. Close to the end, he asked us to help him sit up. I sat next to him on the bed with my right arm around his shoulders and supported him. At 11:08 p.m. there were one, two, three jerks in his body, and he left with the breath. I could physically feel the soul leave the body."

I listened to her recollection in silent amazement, and thanked her for confiding in me something so personal to her and so obviously profound. After Swamiji's leaving, the decision about where we would go and what we would do was truly on us. In reality, that is the way things had always been. It was just nice to check every now and again to see if we were going in the right direction.

Left to our own devices, Carol asked, "What shall we do?"

"Maybe I'll do a practice to get a bit clearer about what we should do."

"So what do you expect a mantra practice is going to do? This doesn't seem very practical."

"Yeah, I know, but It seems that I have to do something, and maybe it's this."

I really hoped a practice would somehow bring clarity. I searched through one of our traditions primary Tantric texts, *Saundaryalahari,* a sourcebook for *Sri Vidya* (knowledge of *Sri,* the divine) and found a verse that touched my heart, a verse related to attaining knowledge of the inner reality.

I sat on my meditation cushion and turned my mala past thirty-three rudraksha seeds every day for thirty-three days, reciting the verse in Sanskrit which translates:

May everything that I do with the sense of self-dedication be items in your service – my conversation, the utterance of your mantra; the movements of my hand, the gestures of your worship; my walking, your circumambulation; my eating, fire-sacrifice to you; the stretching of my body in sleep and rest, prostration to you; and all my enjoyments, offerings made to you.

On the heels of practicing this beautiful verse came an unexpected answer in a dream.

"Carol, I think we have an answer to our problem."

"What is it?"

"Swamiji came in a dream, and we were in Indianapolis."

"Do you know what this means?"

"Yeah, it's Baba giving us instructions."

"But Baba has left his body, he is not here anymore."

My breath stopped. "You know, maybe that is one meaning of the words on the picture in the tea lounge? I've been trying to understand that quote for years now. "**When this life ends, the mystery of love begins.**"

"Sooo . . . what else happened in the dream?"

Yeah, yeah, Baba and I were in momma's kitchen washing dishes."

"Washing dishes?"

"Yep, he was washing and I was drying. He was answering all the unanswered questions I had about practice, you know, the kinds of things that you never got a chance to ask him, or you forgot to ask when you were with him."

"What kinds of things did you ask?"

"I said to him, 'Baba, I know that you can give me *shaktipata* (passing of spiritual energy), but I also know that if I am ill prepared it would be like taking a hit of acid. I would have an experience, but then I'd come back to my same confused self. Am I correct on this?'"

"What'd he say?"

He said, "Yes, sonny, if you have not prepared yourself properly with sincere efforts in meditation, then *shaktipata* would be just like that, an acid trip that you would return from without much permanent effect afterwards."

"Was that a surprise?"

"Well, yeah, but that wasn't all the dream was about."

"Well, I hope not. That information doesn't help us make any practical decision."

"Amid all these questions, a young man suddenly entered the room and interrupted our conversation. The man was showing me aerial photos of land and a building. This young man and I began a dialogue.

"I don't remember what we were saying, but I do know that for a moment, I removed my attention from Baba. When I turned to get his reassurance about interacting with this young man, he was gone."

"He was gone? Where'd he go? Did the dream end?"

"No, the dream went on. I was upset in the dream that I forgot the guru. I was concerned that it said something about getting involved in the world and forgetting my spiritual work."

"Is that what happened?"

"No, no, wait. I went around the house in a panic looking for Baba. For some reason, I looked through the upstairs rooms first, and asked myself where could he have gone? The house was so small. My last place to look was the room next to the kitchen where we'd been washing dishes."

"So you found him in your mother's dining room? No big deal."

"Oh, but it was a big deal. As I walked toward the dining room, I saw him sitting facing me by the door in the living room. He was sitting in deference to someone out of my field of vision. As I walked into the room, there was a woman sitting on the loveseat."

"Was it your mother?"

"No . . . this lovely, but sturdily built, woman, who appeared ageless, and whose presence filled the entire room and more, sat there alone on Momma's loveseat."

"Who do you think the woman was?"

"I . . . I . . . I don't know. When she saw me come into the room, she said, 'You better not let him get away.'"

"In the dream I began hesitatingly, 'Well . . .'"

"Well, what?" Carol said as I choked up a bit.

"Carol, Baba interjected before I could think in the dream and said, 'Oh, no, If I were to go away, he would shed big crocodile tears.'"

This dream was as real as the last interactions Carol and I had with Baba. I had no words to explain what the dream exchange meant to me. What we felt was that we were okayed to begin our work in Indianapolis, and, as usual, in service to the guru, we had no idea what we were really going to learn, or how we would accomplish our ends. He had all the plans.

CHAPTER TWENTY

In the Arms of Grace

*Oh divine Mother, how is it that I can attain the goal
of my life if you do not condescend to grant me pure love
and devotion for thy lotus feet, which are none other
than my own true nature.*

Admittedly, there were times we felt abandoned by the guru and tradition, if for no other reason than the challenge involved in creating something out of nothing, in a wilderness that did not always understand what we had to offer. We fielded many calls, and answered many face-to-face queries from all sorts of people in India. People in this wilderness posed many questions about yoga that I had just never heard before.

One lady, standing at the desk one day, asked, "Do you people teach yoga here, and by that I mean the exercise?"

I started, "Yes, we teach *asana*, but also meditation . . . "

"Stop. I don't want to learn meditation," this harried looking women said. "I don't even want to hear the word meditation mentioned in any classes that I take."

"I'm sorry to offend you. Maybe you have come to the wrong place. For certain you are not required to take meditation, but I can't say that you will never hear the word in a class."

I'd never been confronted by such people before, not even in New York City. Other interactions were just as challenging.

"Can you tell me about your yoga classes?" a black woman on

the other end of the phone asked. "I have high blood pressure, and I need to know if it can help."

I was excited to explain the benefits of yoga to her.

"You know, my graduate work, and research at a hospital was all about the control of blood pressure using yoga. We offer yoga training on multiples levels, and we present it very systematically starting with beginner's cl . . . "

"You're black," she said, interrupting me.

"Excuse me?"

"Yes, you're black. Huh! You couldn't possible know anything about yoga."

What do I say to this woman?

As we sat near the edge of the bed that last morning with Swamiji, he encouraged us, and inspired us.

"When you go home, you will have a little center. You will teach classes, sell books, teach the tradition."

I asked him, "Why are you so intent on us teaching people what we've learned? You've said that yoga is going to become very popular in the future. What does that mean for the tradition? We ran the center in New York. We saw the ebb and flow of people's interest in what you've taught us. Based on that, how are we supposed to support ourselves doing what you ask?"

"What you will do, your work, is for your spiritual growth."

This is going to help my spiritual life? How? How will I be able to gauge my spiritual progress?

The sudden "click" of disconnect and dial tone.

The challenges kept coming. The 1940s Midwest must have been the mindset of the prominent city bank official who responded to our offer of stress management workshops for his bank employees. Our degrees, training, and experience had established us as being preeminently qualified to deliver such programs. But it was here in the twenty-first century that we heard from the human resources manager at the bank.

"Mr. Crenshaw," the manager said to me, rather embarrassed.

"We had been waiting quite expectantly for the okay to do these workshops. The president," the manager went on, "has said that nothing with yoga would ever be offered at his bank. It wasn't Christian."

There was my old friend, religion. I didn't have the words to ask Swamiji questions about these kinds of things at the foot of his bed in January 1996. What nonsense problems had I set up for myself?

In those final instructions there was one piece of information that bore a special fruit.

"Swamiji, proceeding on the path, if I need further instruction in how to help students or myself, from all the elders that I know and respect, around the world, who should I get further instruction or practices from?"

"Son, see Pandit Rajmani," he said, "Panditji knows the tradition."

I had no idea what this meant exactly. Panditji had initiated me into the use of Gayatri mantra while I was in graduate school. Panditji had been the officiating priest at our Vedic wedding ceremony, and he had guided Carol and me both with subtle practices for many years. And so it was Panditji, sitting on our couch one day in Indianapolis, informing Carol and me about a new responsibility.

"Charles-Carol, you should begin to do initiations."

"Initiations?" I couldn't believe what I was hearing, and with the elation came apprehension. Carol and I discussed the revelation after Panditji's departure.

"Carol, can you believe that Panditji's going to train us to be initiators?"

"Initiators are bound in the tradition. This is a fascinating opportunity."

I'd always considered Panditji my elder brother, my elder *guru bhai* (guru brother) in the tradition. As I understood it, only tested mystics, those with a great deal of spiritual understanding, performed this task for the tradition.

Shortly afterwards, after much pondering, came a timely dream, Swamiji with instructions.

"Sit down you two." Carol and I both sat before him, in the dream.

"Okay, let's begin to learn these mantras."

The dream ended. I woke up and wrote down what I remembered, certain now that doing initiations was part of the larger plan that Swamiji had mentioned, a plan that the tradition had for us. Panditji put us through our paces over the course of a few years, and near the end of the preparation, Swamiji came again in a dream.

"Something special is going to happen to Charles and Carol this Christmas!" Swamiji said to some unseen audience in the background, and sure enough, Panditji trained Carol and me in the process of giving *mantra diksha* (mantra initiation) that very Christmas. Swamiji followed up that training with a dream visitation as soon as we returned home from the ashram that Christmas.

"Come," he said, "Let me introduce you to everyone here." There were many people in the room, I couldn't really see any of them, but I knew the introduction was an auspicious event. The dream ended.

The stage was now completely set for us to continue our work with a different impetus, a new energy, something it would take a while to understand fully. Clarity would come in stages, and in strange ways, none more fascinating than a meeting with an African shaman.

My elder guru brothers had suggested I look into the spirituality of the indigenous African traditions and how they related to the religious practices I had grown up with in the United States. More intriguing to me was the connection African indigenous traditions might have with yoga. This was sparked by a conversation with Swamiji, a conversation I'd never mentioned to anyone. "Swamiji? Is India the only place where yoga has existed?" I fully expected someone who had been a *Shankaracharya*, one of the traditional leaders of the Indian religious establishment, to give me a hearty, "But of course!"

He said, "Don't ever think that. It's just that at this point in time India happens to be the custodian of the information. One of my lives was in Egypt, in Africa."

I was astounded, and befuddled, by these words when I heard

them. Recalling what he said drove me to read about the experience and knowledge of African shamans. I found my way to two prominent ones with works written in English, Credo Mutwa and Patrice Malidoma Some. After reading Malidoma's book, *Of Water and the Spirit*, I discovered that he was in the U.S., and I spoke with his secretary about meeting him.

I had no idea where this request was headed, but there was a force propelling me to set up a meeting with this man. Of course, there were lots of people who wanted to see this busy, black African man with two PhDs and an extraordinary tale that was too much like the stories in tantric texts to be overlooked.

"Well, you can't just meet him," the secretary said. "He is traveling the world teaching." "Okay, so if I can't just meet him, then what do I do?"

"Where did you say you lived?"

"I live and work in Indianapolis."

"Well, you are in luck. He is going to be part of a program in Louisville, Kentucky, in November."

"That's just down the road from where I am. I can meet him, or not meet him there?"

"He'll be doing divinations. Would you like to have a divination?"

"What is a divination?"

"Well, he looks at cowry shells and reads your destiny, advises you on your life's work or goals."

I wasn't sure about the divination, but I did want to meet the man. It was my chance to get an insight into how indigenous spiritual people functioned in the world, and how that related to yoga. Up for the adventure, I said, "Okay sign me up for one. If this is the only way I am going to be able to be alone with him, fine."

Louisville was a two-hour ride straight south of Indianapolis. My expectations were mixed as I entered his cozy hotel room at Louisville's Galt House, with my list of questions, questions that would never see the light of day. Malidoma, a highly refined man, dressed in an African print shirt and business casual pants, ushered me into his receiving room slash sleeping quarters.

After the usual pleasantries between strangers, and the formal exchange of fee for services, we sat on the floor between his bed and the window, which overlooked the Ohio River. We sat on either side of a large, white cloth covered with symbols, spread on the floor with a pile of cowry shells, mixed with what appeared, at first glance, to be pieces of junk, sitting in its center. The shaman withdrew into silence.

"You see this pile of shells and symbols," he said as he looked up, "Move them around in a circle."

"Like this?" as I began to move the small, cream-colored snail shells and other small objects clockwise on the circle.

"Yes, yes, that is good. Now stop." His English was impeccable for a French speaker, hardly any accent.

"Wow," he said, "You're off the chart."

"What do you mean, off the chart?" I said puzzled.

He looked puzzled and went on to explain the significance of a few objects that lay before us mixed in with the cowry shells on a symbolic representation of the world.

"It seems that you are here ahead of your time."

"Huh?"

"Well, it means that the mind-made barriers of religion and race make no sense to you. They are not real to you. Has that caused you any problems?"

"You could say that."

I wondered how he was gathering such information from the hodge-podge of items before us on the floor.

"Then there is this I see in the shells here," pointing at some curious object, "But then, I don't have to look at the shells. I can see behind you."

"See behind me?" I looked over my shoulder. All I saw was the soft chair that I was leaning against and the wall.

"Yes. There are people there with white robes, behind you, helping you it seems."

"Hmmm?"

"I am fascinated by how they got here," he said, "Did they come with you or did you call them?"

After a bit of thought I said, "I said a prayer requesting guidance from my tradition for this meeting."

"Ahhh, I see. You've called them here."

"Well, no, I didn't call them here," certain to make no claims of any skills I didn't have. I didn't know how what he saw got there.

"Well, in essence you did call them. There's a piece here that refers to the kind of magic that you carried with you into this life and the responsibility involved with that."

Is he talking about of reincarnation, rebirth? Is this part of African indigenous teaching?

A question I was too flabbergasted to ask.

"What do you mean?"

"You're already in conscious touch with it. That magic is not outside of you, it is IN YOUR BONES."

"Okay."

"Now, there's something here that's challenging for me to explain. Why did you take this particular shape, this particular form. You didn't have to. As a person who is off the human cycle, you didn't have to."

"What do you mean by 'off the human cycle'?"

"Remember in the beginning when I asked you to move the shells around? See this piece?" Malidoma pointed, specifically this time, to an odd little figure on the periphery of the shells and other objects.

"This piece is you. This piece was outside the realm of the world on the chart here. This is what I mean, and there's more."

The chart itself was round with different quadrants and symbols on it.

"What I am trying to understand is why this shape? Why this color? Why did you come here as a black person? It's not clear here. It would make everything so simple."

Malidoma scrutinized his divination objects and chart.

"Yes, yes, why did you choose this form, this garment? The divination objects say that you have this kind of universality, that is the most unlikely thought an African-American would have. You going to the East and sitting with those who are transcendent is a symbol of that. This is the kind of thing that most draws your attention. But it still doesn't explain to me, why this . . . "

"What, what?"

"I just have to say that for myself . . . because . . . because . . . this is the first time I can see that."

"See what?"

"I've never really seen that. I've seen this configuration for other people, but not . . . not . . . from a person, a . . . a black person. So something tells me that your choice was strategic, it has a strategic underpinning, and that somehow it's meant to constitute a statement." I continued to listen to Malidoma in puzzled silence.

"What statement is it, what strategies are you implementing? That's in the shade here, I can't see it here in the shells. The universality in you is how you see the world. What I do know is that who you are is where the world is headed. It has taken thousands of years, and you, you've come here already there. You are a person of the future . . . "

"Explain what you mean." Still puzzled at Malidoma's pronouncements, I questioned how much his insight extended.

"I see here two pieces stuck inside this ring, one male, one female."

"I am a twin, I have a twin sister."

"Ahhh, that explains something. Somehow you needed to merge the gender energy, be an embodiment of the male and female energy, for a better understanding of the human condition. That's why you had to walk out into this world with someone else. . . . You are the embodiment of the human race."

"This is all very interesting. I understand some of it, but some is very confusing."

"Yes, I know that you understand the basics of what I've said, but that's the best I can do. I feel a bit intimidated. I don't talk to people who are not of this earth, they talk to me."

"What do you mean by that?" I was sounding like a two-year-old by now with my questions.

"I don't really have words for it. You see this symbol here?" Malidoma pointed to another object on the chart. "Deep down inside yourself, and I'm going to use your vocabulary here, is a built-in mantra. We'll call it a key, a key that opens space."

"A key?"

"Yes, and I have only seen this key in gatekeepers. Gatekeepers are those who go to the cave, say a sentence, and you hear things collapsing on the other side of the granite rock. All of a sudden, a little being wobbles his way out and says, 'Why did you call me?' You have that key inside you. You have the power of a gatekeeper. With that, I have said enough."

His final remarks brought me back to the realm of where we sat. I thanked Malidoma for his time and left his room. I had only intended to learn something about indigenous African spirituality and yoga. The shaman had unknowingly helped me put pieces of my life together, pieces that previously had only seemed vaguely connected. *What had just happened?*

As I made my way down the hallway to the elevators, the words of the men, the spiritual giants that I most admired, came rushing forward. Memories, my memories of the words they said, like the words that left Gandhi's lips at the moment of his assassination— He Ram (Oh God)—and then the tears welled in my eyes when I remembered Dr. Martin Luther King Jr. and Nelson Mandela's pictures like satellites around Gandhi's, at Gandhi's museum in New Delhi. Dr. Martin Luther King's words rang out: "I've looked over, and I've seen the Promised Land. . . . Mine eyes have seen the glory of the coming of the Lord," words from his very last speech. And then, those famous last words from his "I Have a Dream" speech: "Free at last, free at last, thank God Almighty . . . !" These words took on a completely new power, a meaning that I had quietly considered ever sinse I'd first heard them, but had never voiced.

Dr. King's words were more to me than slogans for the Civil Rights movement; they had always touched something deeper in me. They had always been words that stoked my memory of unity and harmony, something that transcended the smallness of our human minds. His words smacked of a philosophy I was familiar with now, a philosophy that nurtured the ideas of quantum physics, a philosophy that said that everyone, everything comes from an indivisible whole. A philosophy that went by such names as *Sri Vidya,*

Yoga, Tantra, Advaita Vedanta, or Buddhist, as well as the simple reality of the world's indigenous peoples.

My mind drifted to my experience of oneness in my youth, my experience with yoga and my guru. Things had come full circle, against all the odds. That which I sought, I had come with. This was the heart and soul of the yoga I knew and loved. This was the heart and soul of the divine plan. The wise teach that we are all the same, sparks of one transcendent, all-pervading reality, drops, in an ocean of bliss. In truth, we are all great souls, but stranded with our illusion of separateness, we cherish dreams of peace. We cherish these dreams until we go in search of, and find, our true nature, that which we have come with, no matter what path that takes.